7

C000183779

Fanatical *about* Number Plates

Fanatical about Number Plates

The Personalised Number Plate Market today and the stories behind why people buy them

Published by *Regtransfers.co.uk*

Written, edited and compiled by *Ruby Speechley*

The moral right of *Ruby Speechley* to be identified as author of this work, pursuant to section 77 of the Copyright, Designs and Patents Act 1988, is hereby asserted.

Copyright (c) Registration Transfers Ltd 2002

ISBN   0 9543091 0 3

Published by *Regtransfers.co.uk*

Printed by *Rapid Print of Dunstable*

Address: 139 High Street South Dunstable Bedfordshire LU6 3SS

Sales Hotline: 01582 477333 (open 8am - 11pm, 7 days a week)

Wants List Hotline: 01582 600270 (Mon - Fri 9am - 5pm)

Email: sales@regtransfers.co.uk Web: www.regtransfers.co.uk

Acknowledgements

With Special Thanks to:

Noël Woodall

Robert Wicken

John Harrison

Pat Newall (for the late Les Newall)

Steve Waldenberg

Rod Lomax

Max Tyler (of the British Music Hall Society)

Lee Stanley

The Walker Family (for the late Rob Walker)

Stondon Transport Museum

Brocket Hall

Backstage Fancy Dress

Beaulieu Motor Museum

Hulton-Getty Picture Collection

The British Museum Newspaper Library

Peter and Maria Speechley

Richard Pearson

Austen Poole

Tony Johnson

and everyone who has kindly contributed to this book.

Contents

Part One
Introductions

Part Two
Useful Information

Part Three
Plate History - from then to now

Part Four
The Fun Begins - and never ends

Part Five
Lists and Addresses

12

Part One
Introductions

Introduction by Tony Brown, founder of Regtransfers.co.uk.

Foreword by Noël Woodall, co-editor of 'Car Numbers'

What is The Cherished Numbers Dealers Association?

Why was The Registration Numbers Club established?

Permissions

▶ Articles on pages 52-62 and 94-96 by kind permission of John Harrison.

▶ Extracts on pages 54, 85-86, 87-88, 89-90, 91-92 and 93 from *A History of Motor Vehicle Registration in the United Kingdom* by kind permission of Pat Newall on behalf of the author, the late Les Newall.

▶ Extracts from The Times, 1903 - 1904 on pages 67-68, 70, 71 and 72 by kind permission of The British Library.

▶ Extracts from The Autocar on pages 66 and 73 by kind permission of Tony Johnson.

▶ Extracts from The Car Illustrated on pages 67, 74, 75, 76, 77, 78, 79, 80, 81, 82 and 84 by kind permission of John Harrison (Collection held at Beaulieu Library).

▶ Photograph on page 98 by kind permission of the Hulton Getty Picture Collection.

▶ Photographs on pages 52, 63 and 76 by kind permission of Beaulieu Motor Museum.

▶ Photographs on pages 35 and 156 by kind permission of The Stondon Transport Museum.

▶ Photographs on pages 53, 54, 55, 56, 57, 58, 72, 83 and 90 by kind permission of Peter Speechley.

▶ Photographs on pages 278 and 279 by kind permission of Rod Lomax, RNC Club.

▶ Photograph on page 22 by kind permission of Steve Waldenberg RNC Club.

▶ Graham Cox and John Harrison for the Diplomatic plates on page 296.

Introduction

by Tony Brown

This book marks the 100th year of British car registrations. From the very beginning there was a desire to own a 'good-looking' plate. This enthusiasm has never disappeared and many people who enjoy number plates today will have fond memories of spotting the best car numbers around when they were children.

Each time the system changes, there is a renewed interest in the numbers of the previous era, and true to form, this is happening again since the introduction of the seven character combinations in September 2001. Marks like A 1 and N 1 will always be amongst the most sought after because apart from being antiques and two of the first to be issued, they are also 'number one's' and will look incredible on a Fiesta or a Ferrari.

I have had a fascination with cars and number plates from a very young age. In the early 1980's I was a disillusioned young apprentice at Vauxhall Motors in Luton when I began to come up with ideas for starting my own business. It soon became apparent to me that there was a growing market in finding and selling good quality numbers. The first tentative months of Registration Transfers began from my bedroom, and soon moved to small premises. I never envisaged that 20 years later I would be employing around seventy full time staff and that my company would have become the largest cherished numbers dealer in the UK.

This growth and expansion has been due to my belief in re-investing in the company at every level. We strive to keep in line with new technology, ensuring that we are constantly reaching unexplored market places. The very nature of the Internet has taken selling into a whole new arena for us - it makes numbers more accessible to thousands of new customers every week.

Regtransfers has been a pioneer in opening up the market place to those who thought they could never afford to own a personalised number. This book focuses on those people. As you read through their stories, you will see that there are numerous reasons why people choose a particular plate and what it means to them. It illustrates how car numbers have become an intrinsic part of our expression of individuality.

Foreword

by Noël Woodall

C ar registrations, car marks, cherished numbers, personalised registrations, distinctive marks or merely car numbers - call them what you will, they now form a flourishing industry.

The Treasury has benefited by tens if not hundreds of millions of pounds. No longer content with just the transfer fees from these numbers, the DVLA has entered the selling market with much gusto. Its auctions, initially proposed as two or three times a year events (of acceptable classic numbers) have developed into almost monthly auctions of the most dreadful combinations imaginable, and then of course the DVLA also offers a daily telephone service for present day issues.

For me, the interest in personalised numbers began back in 1962 when driving into Blackpool, I saw **BB 4** on a car. Curious to know who owned it, I went to the local library only to be told that there were no books about car numbers available.

I decided to remedy this situation and right away sent out 2,000 circulars to television celebrities, town halls, embassies and most of the entrants in "Who's who". The response was amazing. Owners had been waiting sixty years to tell someone about their choice of number. I quickly learned that **FLY 1** was owned by Lord Brabazon, who held the first pilot's certificate. An estate agent owned **EST 8** and **CUR 10** was owned by an antiques dealer. **SPY 999** was being run by the author of the "I SPY" series of books. Hundreds of other exciting revelations began to pour in, and so the first book in the series of "Car Numbers" was published in 1962 and we coined the words "autonumerology" and "autonumerologist".

My bonus in all this has been the huge numbers of wonderfully interesting letters, many from celebrity owners, which I have received over the past forty years. Many of these I have kept and filed away and now have a considerable collection of celebrities' signatures.

By 1971 the interest in personalised registrations had reached such a peak that a number of number plate dealers got together to form the Personalised Numbers Dealers Association with Dave Kempson doing most of the ground work. The main objective of this organisation was to formalise a standard of trading. Two years later the P.N.D.A. changed its name to the Cherished Numbers Dealers Association. The Institute of Registration Agents and Dealers has also been formed, and I have the privilege of being its chairperson.

Things were going smoothly for owners and dealers until 1976 when the Swansea

Regtransfers.co.uk

dispute tried to stop any future transfers. Following public campaigns, various rallies and even protest marches, the transfer system was finally re-instated in 1977, but unfortunately with many inane rules. For example, it became necessary for a number to have been on a vehicle for at least nine months before it could be transferred. Both vehicles had to be owned (on paper) by the same person and both vehicles had to have an M.O.T.

It was during this dispute that the Registration Numbers Club was formed, initially to combat bureaucratic mayhem. It has now evolved into a strong and friendly association of enthusiasts. They produce a quarterly magazine and organise one of the few remaining number plate rallies each year. Everyone interested in personalised numbers would undoubtedly find membership in this club well worthwhile.

Today the DVLA works more harmoniously with dealers and invited them to a meeting to discuss the introduction of the current system of registrations which started in August, 2001. At that time everyone was convinced that finding saleable combinations would be virtually impossible, but there have been some notable exceptions such as **DE51 RED**, this being one of the first to be bought. The Treasury must still be smiling.

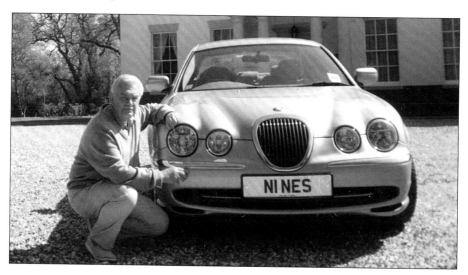

I have been asked many times what personalised marks I have had. There have been many, but those that I have found most difficult to part with were **O 11**, **K 1**, **W 3** and **W 6** . Best of all, perhaps was **XMA 5**; Christmas being my birthday, but I found it hard to live with.

This book is being produced in the one-hundredth year of car registration plates. May the system continue to provide decades more enjoyment for all enthusiasts and may this book contribute also to that enjoyment. I wish it every success.

The CNDA

by Robert Wicken

Personalised and attractive number plates have become a growth industry over the last thirty years, with thousands of motorists now displaying registrations which perhaps represent their initials or advertise their business or profession. Others choose a number which bears an amusing message or simply to disguise the true age of their vehicle.

But to anyone who is not familiar with the complex system of buying, selling, or valuing, personalised registrations in the secondary market, it can contain a number of pitfalls and difficulties.

The Cherished Numbers Dealers Association (CNDA) was established in 1971 to represent reputable and responsible dealers of personalised and attractive registration numbers and to protect the interests of their customers. In 1993 the CNDA became affiliated to the Retail Motor Industry Federation, whose various federated associations represent almost every sector of the retail motor industry.

Members of the CNDA adhere to a strict Code of Practice, and each member is regularly monitored by the Association to ensure that, for instance, members do not advertise registrations that they cannot be reasonably certain of supplying and that transfers are completed within an acceptable time limit. CNDA member dealers have a proven reputation and, in the unlikely event of a problem or dispute, help is close at hand from the CNDA or via the R M I 's free independent conciliation service.

Although you can arrange the transfer of a registration number yourself by direct application to Vehicle Registration Offices, the process of finding a suitable registration and then ensuring that all the legal and Department of Transport requirements are complied with can make the whole business complex and time consuming. Opting for a dealer with CNDA membership assures you of their proven experience and efficiency in handling the formalities for you.

If you decide to sell your registration you will not only need to find a buyer, but also be certain that your number qualifies for transfer and that both donor and recipient vehicles are suitable and in sufficiently good order to enable them to participate in the transfer.

With all this to consider, it may be simpler to let a CNDA expert carry out the work on your behalf.

The Registration Numbers Club

by Rod Lomax

The Registration Numbers Club (RNC) was founded in 1977 and is the only UK based club for cherished number enthusiasts. It is dedicated to preserving the right to hold and transfer cherished vehicle registration numbers, a right which has been held since 1903 and which was once withdrawn in 1977 by the then DVLC following a strike by civil servants at its Swansea headquarters.

The unrealistic and poorly publicised deadline for notifying DVLC of numbers that were residing on old unused vehicles with the old style 'log book' had passed before many people realised it, which unfortunately led to many classic numbers being lost forever.

Things are, however, much different today with DVLA having marketed its own range of numbers for several years, leading to an increased public awareness of the endless possibilities available (whilst also coining it in for HM Government!)

Way back in 1977 the clubs founder, Alex Jackson of Leeds, was so concerned about the situation that he joined forces with classic car enthusiast and club magazine printer, Steve Waldenberg, to form the Registration Numbers Club. Membership quickly soared and the club soon became a voice for the cherished registration enthusiast around the UK.

The club went from strength to strength, holding annual rallies at various venues throughout the country - the cherished number owners voices had been heard and notice had been taken.

Things eventually settled down for the better and the situation regarding registration transfers improved with Local Vehicle Licencing Offices eventually offering a much better and faster service - so much so that today a registration can be transferred in a matter of days rather than months.

Eventually settling down to a membership level of around 500+, the club continues to monitor DVLA activities, although, in reality, there are few problems arising today. It publishes a quarterly newsletter, RNC News, which contains articles and photographs contributed by members as well as news concerning registrations and forthcoming events.

Still prepared by club Organising Secretary, Steve Waldenberg, from the RNC Office in Leeds, 'RNC News' is the only regular publication to deal exclusively with cherished registrations. Long time member, William Heaton, also of Leeds became the club's Publicity Officer in the mid nineties and commenced activities to gain it a higher profile. Unfortunately he had to stand down and Rod Lomax, from Bury in Lancashire, also a long time member, became Publicity Officer in the summer of 2000.

The club celebrated its 20th Anniversary in 1997 with a well attended dinner at Boroughbridge prior to the annual rally at Harewood House, and this year (2002) its 25th anniversary was marked with a rally at Stanford Hall in Leicestershire on Sunday 30 June 2002 with a dinner the previous evening.

Members hold a very wide variety of interesting cherished numbers and it is difficult to single out anyone in particular as they all have their own significance to their owners. However, some of the more memorable ones are, PA6 (Peter Allison from Sheffield), WYN1 (Wyn Calvin from Cardiff), 1U (John Hudson from Stafford), BOY1 (Jason Wilkes from Wolverhampton) and T4 (Colin Richards from Solihull). RNC Honorary Member Noël Woodall from Blackpool and publisher of the Car Numbers range of publications owns N3.

To join the RNC please request a membership application form and sample newsletter etc. from:-
Rod Lomax, RNC Office,
P O Box MT12,
Leeds LS17 7UD.
Tel : 0113 226 7497
Fax: 0113 226 1110.
Email: organisation@registrationnumbersclub.org.uk

RNC Club Members Cars and plates
Dean Easterby - 1 DLE and Michael Farquharson - B7 TCH

Part Two
Useful Information

Having your mark valued

How to protect the rights to your plate

Why are number plates such a lucrative investment?

The new style registration system explained

Your questions answered

Regtransfers place in today's market

Registration Transfers was established in 1982 by Tony Brown, from Dunstable, Bedfordshire. He started the business in his bedroom, and 20 years on, Tony has turned his dream into the largest number plate dealer in the U.K. Now employing over 60 staff, half of which are sales people, the company owns thousands of number plates. Tony Brown has truly positioned Regtransfers as the market leader in buying and selling quality personalised number plates.

Registration Transfers recently adopted its website address, regtransfers.co.uk, as its new name. Constantly being updated and improved, Regtransfers is the first port of call for anyone interested in finding their ideal number. Regtransfers is the first choice of famous celebrities such as Robbie Williams, Chris Eubank, Prince Naseem Hamid, Frank Warren, DJ Pied Piper, Willie Carson, Iwan Thomas, Katharine Merry, Jamie Baulch, Sid Owen (Ricky in Eastenders), Kriss Akabussi and Max Bygraves.
Some of the categories set up to help customers find what they are looking for are: Mr Numbers, Birthdays, Naughty Numbers, Football, Executive Collection and Plates Like Names. The unique Supersearch® facility promises to 'Find a number plate for everyone'.

Regtransfers now dominates the number plate sections in many national newspapers and car magazines, such as: *Daily Telegraph, Sunday Times, Exchange and Mart, Top Gear, What Car?* and *AutoTrader.* This domination now extends right across the Internet, thus ensuring excellent exposure for the

many thousands of private individuals selling their plates through the company.

What makes Regtransfers different from the rest?

Together with over 20 years experience, one of the secrets of Regtransfers success has been its ability to maintain the highest standards of customer care at all times.
This first class, caring service not only includes finding the best number plate to suit the individual needs of the customer, but also handling the transfer paperwork, thus taking the worry out of the customers hands.

Renowned for listening to customers needs, Regtransfers has recently extended its hours of business from 8am to 11pm 7 days a week. This unprecedented move illustrates Regtransfers willingness to evolve and reinvest in the business. Regtransfers also constantly updates it's computer system to ensure an efficient and reliable service.

With access to millions of number plates through their vast database, Regtransfers' highly trained sales staff can find the customer a suitable number plate in seconds. They will also search for any similar number plates so that the customer is fully aware of all the possibilities available to them.

If the plate they are looking for is not available the Sales Person will suggest other plates to fit in with a different area of their life - ones which the customer may not have previously considered.

Regtransfers.co.uk

They will also suggest that their details are passed onto the 'Wants List' department who will keep their details on a database. As soon as a matching number plate becomes available, the client will be offered first refusal.

The Regtransfers Marketing Department produce a full colour 24 page brochure every month. It is the largest brochure produced by any Cherished Number Plate Dealer. By filling in a form on the website, a copy will be dispatched within 48 hours.

What are Cherished Number Plates all about?

Commonly misunderstood by many, personal or 'cherished' number plates can now sell for more than the average priced house. On 10th December 1993 an anonymous buyer paid a staggering £235,000 for their ultimate numberplate: 'K1 NGS' (Kings). It took the auctioneer just over two minutes to achieve this figure. Other examples of registrations that have sold for large amounts of money are: '1 A' £202,000; 'S1 NGH' (Singh) £108,000; '1 RR' £106,000; 'G1 LLY' (Gilly) £87,500; 'P1 LOT' (Pilot) £82,500 & 'ELV 1S' (Elvis) £75,000.

Thankfully not all registration marks are so expensive. Many start from around £250, plus a transfer fee of £80. Love them or hate them, personal number plates are becoming more and more popular. For example, businesses use them as another form of advertising their company, like the top bed firm in Oxford, *And so to Bed* who purchased the number plate CO51 BED from Regtransfers for their company delivery van. Even Lorry drivers like to hang a second plate on their vehicles, next to their registration number, often with their nickname printed out - perhaps as the next best thing to a real name plate.

Kriss Akabussi sees the fun side of number plates.

Most commonly, people want a personalised plate as a mark of their success in life or simply to adorn their favourite vehicle.

Customers are increasingly purchasing number plates as an investment for themselves, their children and family. They are now considered a serious alternative to Baby bonds and ISA's.

Who buys Personal Number Plates?

People from every walk of life buy personal number plates. The most publicised are of course television and sports personalities. They buy them for a variety of reasons such as for self-recognition and promotional purposes, for example many footballers have chosen to buy their initials or name plates from Regtransfers: Emile Heskey, Andy Cole, David Seaman, Ashley Cole, Roy Keane, Stan Collymore, Chris Waddle, Steve Staunton, David Pleat, Steve Claridge, Barry Venison and Bobby Robson.

They have become the ultimate accessory for every car owner and with the huge variety of plates available at very reasonable prices - there really is an affordable plate for everyone.

The most popular choices are for peoples names, initials, the name of a hobby or even the name or breed of pet, for instance: 'CAT 1'; 'A800 PUG'; 'A9 DOG'; 'S4 NDY' (Sandy); '1 UCY' (Lucy); 'T6 NYA' (Tanya); '1 EO' (Leo); 'C1 LLA' (Cilla); 'M4 TCH' (Match); 'B1 RDY' (Birdy) and '50 NGS' (Songs), MS 1, TB 4 and 9 RR.

A Serious Investment

"If" you buy your number wisely, it will honestly be better than money in the bank," said Quentin Willson in BBC Top Gear Magazine. Indeed many investment markets cannot claim to "buck the trend", but one exception over the last 10 years has been the Cherished Number Plate industry.

In 20 years of trading at Regtransfers, we have found that values of number plates are increasing year on year. Investing in this market place is fast becoming recognised as a sound financial move.

Number plates have been bought and sold since the 1960's, but it has only been in more recent years that their values have massively increased. Many of our clients have valuable collections of numbers that they enjoy on a personal level as well as the financial security they can bring. These plates are often passed on to loved ones in their wills, as an important part of their estate.

With the combinations changing every six months now, there is plenty of opportunity to invest in the new numbers as well as the old. Some of our clients are thinking up words and names for the new style number plates, buying up several, then selling them on at a profit. Many clients take a long-term view and compile hugely valuable collections over many years. Even if you only have one on a car the other numbers can be held safely on retention certificates.

Some examples of cherished number plate prices are shown opposite, illustrating the current value against the cost when first purchased.

Although this is only a small selection it shows the immense increase in cherished registration values over the last 10 years. Investing in personalised numbers is certainly not the most obvious of choices, but it is becoming a serious proposition to businessmen and investors alike.

'Number One' plates such as 1 NU, name plates such as 1 UCY and pairs of plates such as 1 WET and WET 1 are the types of plates which are the most desirable, thus the most likely to increase in value.

At Regtransfers.co.uk, we are able to offer our clients sound, expert advice and guidance when selecting number plates for this purpose. Many are already enjoying the rewards from this mid to long term investment, at the same time enjoying having a personal plate on their vehicle.

Registration	Date of Sale	Price Then	Current Market Value
1 NU	1995	£2,400	£25,000
1VV	1995	£5,800	£20,000
WKS 1	1994	£2,200	£12,000
1 TCB	1992	£3,000	£15,000
NSH 1	1994	£2,600	£15,000
PAU 1Y	1996	£3,000	£20,000
1 OY	1994	£3,400	£25,000
1 OA	1992	£3,200	£17,500
HPS 1	1994	£3,300	£12,500
1 SAJ	1995	£3,300	£12,500
1 YF	1998	£4,000	£22,500

Ivan Scott enjoys investing in numbers (see full story page 177)

Valuing your Mark

Pricing the registration is the most important factor when trying to sell a cherished number. You therefore need to be aware that some dealers may overprice your number just to get it on their books but without much chance of achieving the price quoted.

As there is no authoritative publications on the subject of number plate valuations, we rely on our 20 years of professional experience to apply a truly realistic valuation taking into account the following:

Age and rareness - how old it is and how many of that series were issued.

How well it will sell - how popular the initials or names are.

The lowness of the number - number 1's are the most sought after.

Cross reference - using our computer networks to compare similar registrations on the market.

Price trends - taking into consideration prices achieved in the past, at present and at auction.

When you use the valuation service at Regtransfers, we take into consideration all the above points and more. This should result in the best chance of a sale at the current market value.

We pride ourselves on our quick, helpful and efficient service, so if you are serious about selling, give us a call and leave the rest to us.

Protect your Rights

It is possible to lose the right to your registration number and for the DVLA to claim it back. It happens to people every year because they fail to understand the registration rules.

There are two ways of owning the right to a registration:

1. Having the plate registered to a vehicle.
2. Retaining the registration on retention certificate.

It is imperative to safeguard your rights to a registration once purchased. Rights to a number are held by the registered keeper shown on a V5 or the name indicated at the top of a retention document (if not currently assigned to a vehicle).

Before selling or scrapping a vehicle, the mark must be transferred to another vehicle in your name or put on retention. Failure to do so will result in the loss of this registration. It is also advisable to check with the DVLA should you be exporting your vehicle, as failure to adopt the correct procedure could also mean the loss of your number.

For the registration to be transferred the donor vehicle must have a current V5 and MOT certificate (if applicable - for vehicles older than 3 years). The road fund licence (tax disc) must be current or have been so within the last six months and have expired naturally (not cashed in). The receiving vehicle must have a V5 and a current MOT (if applicable) and be taxed (although the tax can be obtained at the same time as the transfer is carried out).

It is also possible to lose your rights to a registration if you fail to renew a retention document when due. The duration is one year and can only be renewed within 28 days of expiry for a fee of £25.

Finally, illegal display of your number plate can lead to losing the rights to your number.

Insurance & Risk

In 1983 it became legal to transfer a registration from a stolen vehicle. This is as long as the vehicle is reported stolen to the police and not recovered for a minimum of one year from that date. Selected Insurance companies offer cover for the period of loss.

You will not lose your entitlement to your registration if your vehicle is in an accident and written off. Just make sure that you make an application to your nearest Local Office immediately to transfer the registration to another vehicle or retention certificate. Waiting for the insurance company to pay you could result in **them** becoming the new owner instead of you.

You will need a letter from your insurance company stating the number plate, chassis number and confirmation that the vehicle is written off and that the insurance company have no rights to your number. Failure to do this could result in the right to apply for a transfer passing to them. If this happens, you will lose all your rights to the number.

We advise that you should never formally surrender your ownership of the vehicle until the transfer has been processed at the DVLA and that you have the new vehicle registration document or retention certificate in your possession.

On occasions the LO will ask to inspect the donor vehicle to ensure that it exists and to examine its chassis number to ensure that is corresponds with the information records.

For further information see the section 'All you need to know about Registration Numbers - Your Questions Answered' on page 43.

Housed at the Stondon Transport Museum, this 1954 Austin A40 Somerset was, in its day, a very popular family car which soon became known for its reliability. To prove this point, Austin arranged for one of these vehicles to be driven from the Arctic circle to the Equator and this was achieved without mishap - a distance of some 8,000 miles.

This particular vehicle is one of the last Austin A40s made and is the last Austin car built on a separate chassis. It is powered by a 1200cc engine with a four speed gearbox. The price when new was £467.

GVS 334 was issued in Greenock. This wouldn't have been the car's original number though, as all GVS numbers were replacement numbers.

The new registration system for Great Britain was introduced on 1st September 2001. It replaces the old prefix system which ended on 31st August 2001 with the 'Y' registrations. The new format is made up of three parts:

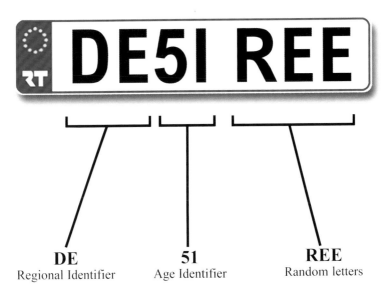

DE
Regional Identifier

51
Age Identifier

REE
Random letters

Regional Identifier - A two letter Regional Identifier. The first letter represents the region and the second letter relates to a Local Office.

Age Identifier - A two figure Age Identifier. For example, 51 represents the period between September 2001 and February 2002.

Random letters - Three random letters, including for the first time, the letter Z.

Regional Identifiers

Local Offices		1st letter	2nd letter
Anglia	Peterborough Norwich Ipswich	A	A-N O-U V-Y
Birmingham	Birmingham	B	A-Y
Cymru	Cardiff Swansea Bangor	C	A-O P-V W-Y
Deeside to Shrewsbury	Chester Shrewsbury	D	A-K L-Y
Essex	Chelmsford	E	A-Y
Forest and Fens	Nottingham Lincoln	F	A-P R-Y
Garden of England	Maidstone Brighton	G	A-O P-Y
Hampshire & Dorset	Bournemouth Portsmouth	H	A-J K-Y
....	Luton Northampton	K	A-L M-Y
London	Wimbledon Stanmore Sidcup	L	A-J K-T U-Y
Manchester and Merseyside	Manchester	M	A-Y
North	Newcastle Stockton	N	A-O P-Y
Oxford	Oxford	O	A-Y

Local Offices		1st letter	2nd letter
Preston	Preston	**P**	A-T
	Carlisle		U-Y
Reading	Reading	**R**	A-Y
Scotland	Glasgow	**S**	A-J
	Edinburgh		K-O
	Dundee		P-T
	Aberdeen		U-W
	Inverness		X-Y
Severn Valley	Worcester	**V**	A-Y
West of England	Exeter	**W**	A-J
	Truro		K-L
	Bristol		M-Y
Yorkshire	Leeds	**Y**	A-L
	Sheffield		M-V
	Beverley		W-Y

Age Identifiers

Year	March to August	September to February
2001		51
2002	02	52
2003	03	53
2004	04	54
2005	05	55
2006	06	56

Age Identifiers

Year	March to August	September to February
2007	07	57
2008	08	58
2009	09	59
2010	10	60
2011	11	61
2012	12	62
2013	13	63
2014	14	64
2015	15	65
2016	16	66
2017	17	67
2018	18	68
2019	19	69
2020	20	70
2021	21	71
2022	22	72
2023	23	73
2024	24	74
2025	25	75
2026	26	76

Year	March to August	September to February
2027	27	77
2028	28	78
2029	29	79
2030	30	80
2031	31	81
2032	32	82
2033	33	83
2034	34	84
2035	35	85
2036	36	86
2037	37	87
2038	38	88
2039	39	89
2040	40	90
2041	41	91
2042	42	92
2043	43	93
2044	44	94
2045	45	95
2046	46	96
2047	47	97
2048	48	98
2049	49	99

All you need to know about Registration Numbers

Your Questions Answered

Q: How should a registration be displayed?

A: Registration numbers must be correctly displayed in accordance with the regulations governing the design, manufacture and display of vehicle registration plates. It is an offence to mis-space or mis-represent registrations on number plates or to corrupt numbers to appear as letters or vice versa. More information on spacing can be found in leaflet V796 Display of Registration Marks which is obtainable from your nearest LO and the Driver and Vehicle Licensing Agency (DVLA), Swansea.

Q: What is a registration number and who has entitlement to it?

A: Registration numbers are not items of property in their own right. They are assigned, and may be withdrawn by the Secretary of State as part of the basic registration and licensing process which is required by law. The registration number is a unique means of identifying a vehicle, primarily for taxation and law enforcement purposes. It is assigned **to the vehicle,** rather than its keeper, and unless it is transferred or retained the registration number normally remains with the vehicle until it is broken up, destroyed or sent permanently out of the country.

An individual acquires entitlement to a registration number when he or she becomes the registered keeper of the vehicle which carries the number. When the vehicle changes hands, entitlement to its registration number will automatically pass with the vehicle to the new keeper unless use is made of the special facilities which have been designed to allow motorists to acquire and retain particular registration numbers. Visit www.regtransfers.co.uk to read about these facilities as well as the Cherished Transfer, Retention and Sale of Marks schemes.

Q: What do I get from the seller for my money?

A: Vehicle Registration numbers are not items of property, so you cannot buy legal title to them. When you "buy" an assigned number, therefore, what you are actually paying for is the agreement of the registered keeper of the vehicle which carries the number to apply to the DVLA to transfer it from his/her vehicle to yours under the Cherished Transfer facility. Once the number has been transferred to your vehicle, you then acquire the entitlement (as the registered keeper of the vehicle) to apply to transfer or retain the number.

Q: How can I safeguard my entitlement to a number?

A: Entitlement to a number is effectively the right of the registered keeper of a vehicle to apply to have the number transferred to another vehicle (either his own or someone else's). The keeper is also entitled to apply to have the number of his vehicle put on retention, that is to say take the number off the vehicle and put it on hold pending re-assignment to another vehicle.

It is important to note that the keeper may apply, but the application will only be granted if all the conditions relating to the retention and transfer facilities are satisfied. You can help to safeguard your entitlement, therefore, by ensuring that your vehicle is able to meet these conditions.

If you no longer have the vehicle which properly displays the number (ie it is in someone else's keepership or has been scrapped, broken up, destroyed or exported) then your entitlement to the number ceases.

Q: What if my vehicle is stolen and not recovered?

A: If your vehicle is stolen and has not been recovered after a year you can apply to have its registration number re-assigned to your replacement vehicle providing certain conditions are met. In order to qualify for the concession, the theft must have been notified to the police and recorded at DVLA as stolen for not less than 12 months. In addition, at the time of the theft the vehicle must have had a current test pass certificate and have had a current vehicle excise licence (tax disc). The Agency will also require a letter from your insurers confirming that they have no objection to the number being re-issued. This must be provided because once insurers have settled your claim, they have a rightful claim to the vehicle should it be recovered. Please also read the IMPORTANT opposite.

To apply, or for further information, write quoting the registration number to:
Cherished Transfer Section, D13,
Driver and Vehicle Licensing Agency,
Swansea SA6 7JL.
If you wish to telephone, DVLA's Customer Enquiries
the number is: (01792) 772134.

Q: What if my vehicle is "written off"?

A: A write-off happens when a damaged vehicle is judged by insurers to be beyond economic repair. In such a case, the insurance company agrees a pay-out with the insured, and legal ownership of the vehicle then passes to the insurance company. The company is then free to sell the vehicle as salvage and the purchaser may repair it and put it back on the road.

If your vehicle is written off, you may still apply to transfer or retain its number providing:

(a) the vehicle is available for inspection and

(b) you can satisfy all the conditions of the transfer or retention schemes

IMPORTANT: It is essential that you discuss your cherished registration number with your insurers at the outset. You will need to ensure they are aware that in the event of a write-off, the vehicle must be made available for inspection by DVLA if you are to transfer or retain the number. If your insurers settle your claim and sell the vehicle as salvage before the number is properly transferred or retained, the mark will pass with the vehicle to the new keeper and you will lose your entitlement. You will also lose entitlement if the vehicle is sent for scrapping before the number is transferred or retained.

Once you have successfully transferred or retained your registration number from the written off vehicle, let your insurers know about the change of number and send them the amended V5 registration document. If your insurers intend to sell the write-off as salvage, the vehicle must display the replacement registration number.

Q: What if my vehicle has been scrapped?

A: Scrapping occurs when a vehicle, whether an insurance write-off or not, is broken up for spares or otherwise destroyed. Once a vehicle ceases to exist its registration number is cancelled.

If your vehicle has been scrapped, you will not be able to transfer its registration number.

The person who actually breaks up or destroys the vehicle must notify the DVLA that the vehicle has been scrapped and return the V5 registration document

Q: What are the Cherished Transfer and retention schemes?

A: The Cherished Transfer Scheme enables an assigned registration number to be moved directly from one vehicle to another. Only the registered keeper of a vehicle is entitled to apply to transfer its number. Application form V317 Transfer of Registration Mark must be completed and the fee for a transfer is £80 (at time of publication).

If the vehicle which is receiving the number in a cherished transfer is already registered, its existing number will become void unless an application to transfer or retain that number is made at the same time.

The Retention Scheme enables a number to be held apart from the vehicle it has been assigned to, for a 12 month period pending its re-assignment to another vehicle. Only the registered keeper of a vehicle is entitled to apply for a right of retention. Application form V778/1 Retention of Vehicle Registration Mark must be completed and the application fee is £25 plus an assignment fee of £80, bringing the total payable to £105 (at time of publication). Successful applicants are issued with a V778 Retention Document, valid for 12 months, which records details of the registration number, the grantee (the applicant), and nominee details where supplied in the application. If, after you have received your document, you wish to add or change nominee details, you will need to apply to DVLA, returning your document together with a fee of £25.

REMEMBER: **The retention right is granted to the applicant (the grantee) alone and it is non-transferable - the nominee has no rights to the number.**

Only the grantee can apply to have the retained registration number assigned, and it can only be assigned to a vehicle which is registered to the grantee, or to the nominee shown on the retention document.

Once you have assigned the retained number to your, or your nominee's vehicle, you have fully exercised your rights under the terms of the retention facility. After assignment, entitlement to the number comes through being the keeper of the vehicle which has received it. Only the keeper is entitled to apply for further retention or transfer of the number.

If the vehicle which is receiving the retained number is already registered, its existing number will become void unless an application to retain or transfer that number is made at the same time.

The V317 and V778/1 forms contain notes for guidance and are available from DVLA and your nearest LO (but see section 1). For the address and telephone number look in your telephone directory under "Transport, Department of".

Before you apply, check your V5 registration Document to make sure that the number is transferable. If it is not, it will say so on the V5. If the registration document states that the registration number is non-transferable, then it cannot be retained either. However, the vehicle may still be eligible to receive a cherished mark (this does not apply if the vehicle has a "Q" mark).

You should also check to make sure that the conditions for the transfer and retention schemes can be compiled with. These conditions are as follows :-

Vehicles must be available for inspection.

The inspection helps to verify entitlement to the registration number being transferred / retained. Both the donor (the vehicle giving up the number) and the recipient (the vehicle receiving the number) may be called for inspection.

Vehicles must be subject to MOT / HGV test. Non-testable vehicles such as agricultural tractors and milk floats, for example, are outside the scope of the schemes. Only testable vehicles can participate in transfers and retentions and valid test certificates must be sent with applications.

Vehicles must be currently licensed, or in the process of being licensed. The application will still be considered, however, where the last licence (tax disc) expired within six months of the date of application, or if the licence has been voluntarily surrendered for refund, the six-month concession does not normally apply.

If you are satisfied that you have met all the conditions, you can send your application to your nearest LO. If everything is in order and the application is approved, a replacement registration number which is appropriate to its age will be assigned. If the vehicle was registered before 1963 it will be assigned a number which does not contain a year identifier and which you will not be able to transfer or put on retention.

Replacement tax disc(s) will be issued, and the MOT certificates(s) - where applicable - will be endorsed to show that the vehicle's number has changed.

Finally, registration document(s) showing the changed registration number will be sent out from DVLA to the keeper(s). In the case of a retention application, a V778 Retention Document, valid for 12 months, will also be sent to the grantee.

IMPORTANT: DO NOT dispose of the vehicle until the application has been fully completed and you have received the amended registration document(s). If you dispose of the vehicle too soon, you may lose entitlement to the cherished mark.

REMEMBER: Once your transfer / retention has been successfully completed, tell your insurers and breakdown company that the vehicle's registration number has changed!

Q: Are there any special rules for motorcycles / mopeds?

A: No.

Q: What if my assignment / retention rights are due to expire and I do not have a receiving vehicle for the number?

A: Approximately 28 days before your rights are due to expire, you should receive a reminder letter from DVLA. It will advise you of the imminent expiry of your rights and offer you the opportunity of purchasing, for a £25 fee, a 12 month extension period. The reminder also contains a special section which you can use to apply for the extension.

IMPORTANT: There is no obligation on the DVLA to send you a reminder. It is your responsibility to know when your rights are due to expire and it is up to you to either assign the number or apply for an extension before this happens. Your rights will be lost if you act too late.

Q: Can I add or change nominee details on my certificate of entitlement / retention document?

A: Yes, providing your certificate / document is current. The fee is £25. Your reminder letter or your new-style Certificate of Entitlement or Retention Document will tell you how to apply.

If you have an old-style Certificate of Entitlement (these contain no information about applying to add or change a nominee) please ask DVLA for application form V750/2. Similarly, if you have an old-style Retention Document please ask DVLA for application form V778/3.

Q: What if I decide that I no longer want the number?

A: You do not have to assign the number if you do not wish to; you can simply allow your assignment / retention rights to expire. You need take no further action unless you paid the (£80) assignment fee when you acquired the rights; in this case you can apply to DVLA for a refund of this fee - your Certificate of Entitlement or Retention Document tells you how.

NOTE: If you allow your rights to expire, you will not be able to recover them at a later date.

You may only apply for refund of the assignment fee after the rights have expired.

You will not be able to apply for refund of the purchase price or the retention fee.

Q: What happens to my registration number if I export my vehicle?

A: You are legally obliged to notify the DVLA if you are taking your vehicle abroad for more than 12 months. More information on this can be found in leaflet V100 which is available from LO's and main Post Offices.

What you need to do to secure the registration number depends on the circumstances. For example, you may be selling the vehicle overseas. In this case, you must either transfer or retain the number before you part with the vehicle. Alternatively, you may be going abroad with the vehicle for a few years and intend to bring it back with you when you return. In this case transfer or retention before you leave is not essential, as most vehicles on return to this country from overseas are able to pick up their GB registration numbers, provided documentary evidence to link the vehicle and the number is available.

The best course of action is to get advice from your local LO, or from Customer Enquiries at DVLA, well in advance of the planned date of export. For the address and telephone number of your local LO look in your telephone book under "Transport, Department of". You can write to Customer Enquiries (Vehicles) at the Driver and Vehicle Licensing Agency, Swansea SA99 1BL. If you wish to telephone, the number you need is 08702 400010.

Please note: If you wish to transfer or retain your number you must do so before the vehicle leaves Great Britain - you cannot apply once the vehicle is out of the country.

Q: I have an old vehicle which is not registered at DVLA. Can I register the vehicle and transfer or retain its registration number?

A: It is possible for the vehicle to be registered at DVLA. But you will not be able to transfer or retain its number.

If you are able to supply documentary evidence (eg the old-style log book) to establish a link between the vehicle and the registration number, you should be able to register the vehicle under that number. If you do not have documentary evidence, or you do not know the vehicle's registration number, the vehicle may still be registered but in this case a number appropriate to its age will be assigned by the DVLA. If the age or origin of the vehicle cannot be established, then the DVLA may register the vehicle under a "Q" number. Whatever the circumstances, however, the vehicle's registration number will be non-transferable. This arrangement helps to safeguard entitlement by removing the incentive there would otherwise be for spurious claims to attractive old registration numbers.

For more details please see leaflet SJ94/96 "How to Register Your Old Vehicle", available from your LO and DVLA.

Q: My vehicle has a "Q" prefix registration number. Can it participate in the transfer and retention schemes?

A: Sorry, no. Vehicles are assigned "Q" prefix registration numbers to draw attention to the fact that their origins or age are uncertain. "Q" numbers are therefore **non-transferable** and must remain with the vehicle unless documentary evidence which confirms its origins / age comes to light. In this case, the evidence should be sent to your nearest LO who may then assign a replacement age-related number to the vehicle.

Q: My V5 registration document says my registration number is non-transferable. Can I transfer a cherished number onto my vehicle?

A: Yes. Although you cannot transfer or retain a non-transferable number, the vehicle can receive a registration number providing the non-transferable number is not a "Q" mark and providing the vehicle meets the normal conditions of the Sales, Transfer and Retention schemes.

Q: I have seen Northern Ireland registration numbers advertised. Can I transfer one onto my vehicle?

A: Yes, providing the donor and recipient vehicles are registered at DVLA or on the NI Register. Similarly, you may transfer a GB number to a vehicle registered in NI. In either case the vehicles must, of course, meet the requirements of the transfer scheme.

Q: I have an old style log book / V5 registration document but the vehicle no longer exists. Can I claim the registration number?

A: Sorry, no. Once a vehicle has ceased to exist, entitlement to its number also ceases. Possession of a log book or registration document alone does not give entitlement to a registration number. If a vehicle has been scrapped, you are required by law to notify the Secretary of State and return the registration document to DVLA.

Part Three
Plate History - from then to now

100 years of British Vehicle Registrations

Extracts from publications at the time

In-depth articles by the late Les Newall

Almost 100 Years of British Vehicle Registrations

by John Harrison

Earl Russell in his Napier with the number plate A 1.

In the beginning

Although it is nearly 100 years old, the British registration system is not the oldest in the world. The first proper registration system appears to have been adopted by the state of Baden in Germany in 1896 and the first country to adopt a national one was Holland in 1899. One distinction of the British system is that a registration issued when it started in 1903 can still be valid on the same vehicle today, though Britain cannot claim the oldest system in this respect. In the Spanish system, an original plate could be valid on the same vehicle that dates back to 1900.

Vehicle registrations were introduced under the provisions of the Motor Car Act 1903. All motor vehicles used on the roads after 1 January 1904 had to be registered with the appropriate local authority. In fact most authorities started issuing registrations towards the end of 1903. One suggestion which had been put forward prior to the passing of the Act was that cars should be given names, in a similar way to ships, rather than numbers. Fortunately, in view of subsequent growth in vehicular traffic, the government did not accept this proposal!

To facilitate the issuing of registrations, local authorities were allocated codes of one or two letters. Codes with G, S or V in them were reserved for Scottish authorities and codes with I and Z in them were reserved for Ireland. England and Wales were allocated the remaining codes. Interestingly, no special recognition was given to Wales' status in the allocation.

English and Welsh codes were allocated alphabetically by size of population. Thus, London, the largest authority, was given A; Lancashire the next largest B, and so on to AA for Hampshire, AB for Worcestershire etc until finally diminutive Rutland received FP. In Scotland the three largest authorities, Glasgow, Edinburgh and Lanarkshire, were allocated the single letters G, S & V respectively. The remaining codes were allocated using alphabetical order of authority name, e.g. SA to Aberdeenshire, SB to Argyll, etc. Irish codes were allocated by alphabetical order of authority name (I & Z were not allocated as single letters), i.e. IA to Antrim, IB to Armagh, etc.

Much recent DVLA publicity refers to A 1 as being the first registration issued. It certainly was the first one issued by London, but it is likely other authorities started issuing registrations slightly earlier than London. In order to be allocated the number A1, Earl Russell had queued all night outside the London CC offices.

It is interesting to note the codes omitted from the original allocation:

BF - standing for Bloody Fool, a then popular acronym. This was originally allocated to Dorset but soon withdrawn in preference to FX. BF, with use restricted to three-letter combinations, was re-allocated to Staffordshire in 1960.

DD - It is understood this was a form of alcoholic deliria, q.v. DT below. The series was commenced by Gloucestershire in 1921.

DF - an acronym for Damned Fool. This was originally allocated to Northampton, but following objections from that Council, the code NH was substituted. DF subsequently went to Gloucestershire in 1926.

DT - standing for delirium tremens. When Doncaster became a separate county borough in 1927, the mark DT was a logical code to allocate to it.

ER - the then royal cypher. Commenced by Cambridgeshire in 1922.

SC, SF, SG, CS, FS & GS were omitted from the Scottish allocation. The likely explanation for this is the possibility of confusing the letters C & G and E and F - at this time most number plates were hand painted, sometimes rather crudely.

Each code was to be followed by a serial number of up to four digits. Local authorities had to keep three separate registers of vehicles; ordinary cars, "heavy motor cars" (lorries and buses in reality) and motorcycles. Some just issued numbers

Pre-number plates. Mr. A.A. Speechley in an 1897 Benz, 1 cyl, 3.5 hp. Photo taken at Churchfield Road, Acton, Middx, early 1930's.

sequentially, not segregating the vehicle types. Others had segregation, either in blocks or by using odd and even numbers for different categories. Some used lead zeros in front of one type of number, e.g. heavy motor cars might have numbers like AB 0123. Some had two or three parallel systems, so there could be two or even three different vehicles with the same numbers!

The System Develops

New codes were generally needed for one of two reasons; either an existing authority was "running out" of available numbers or a new county borough was being created. The early years of the twentieth century were a period of industrialisation and consequent rapid urban growth, so many towns expanded and reached a size justifying separate borough status.

The original 1903 allocation in England and Wales ended at FP (Rutland). The next two codes to be used both went to new boroughs, FR to Blackpool and FT to Tynemouth. FU and FW were omitted (It should be noted that FS and FV were both intended for use in Scotland). It is easy to surmise why FU was omitted, but there is no obvious reason for leaving out FW. As has already been explained, FX was allocated to Dorset as residents of that area objected to having BF as their code.

Not surprisingly, the first authority to use up its original code was London. This was allocated LC in 1905 and LN in 1906. The next authority to require a second code was Middlesex which commenced MX in 1912.

Harefield Road, Uxbridge, Middlesex. Number plate MX 6280. Issued in Middlesex, July 1912.

Three principles appear to have been used in allocating new and further codes. Some were allocated on a mnemonic basis, e.g. LC (London County) and LN to London, MX to Middlesex and KN to Kent. In other cases an attempt was made to give authorities an "alphabetical run" of codes, e.g. most of the LX codes subsequently went to London and Cheshire after being originally allocated M was given MA & MB.

In yet other cases the original alphabetical sequence was followed, e.g. when Merthyr Tydfil was created a separate borough in 1908 it received HB. Eventually it was realised that, with reserving G, S & V

William Newing at Brighton
Number Plate LL-9827. Issued in London, March 1914.

codes for Scotland, this country would be over provided with codes. Thus some codes with G and V in them "came south of the border", the first one being VB allocated to Croydon in 1927, but codes with S in them remained exclusively Scottish until 1974.

The system of registering vehicles was initially much looser than it is today. For instance, if the owner of a vehicle moved to another authority or a vehicle was sold across an authority boundary, it would often be re-registered. The Roads Act of 1920 included among its provisions a tightening up of procedures relating to vehicle registration. The practice of re-registering vehicles which were moved to another authority area ceased. The Act required that a vehicle would now retain its registration for the lifetime of that vehicle.

In 1921 the Irish Free State, now the Irish Republic was established. Perhaps surprisingly, the Irish registration system remained based on the British system until 1987, though when reflective plates were introduced in the Republic rear plates were given a red background whereas in Britain the background was yellow. A convention was agreed whereby in the Republic Zx combinations would be used for new codes and in the North xZ would be used.

Coping with vehicle growth

By 1932 most of the two-letter codes had been allocated and the registration system had to be further developed. The decision was made to add a third letter to the authority's code letters followed by up to three numbers, i.e. ABC 123 format where BC would represent the authority code. Staffordshire was the first authority to move onto three letters, ARF being commenced in July 1932. It is interesting to note that Staffordshire had the codes RE and RF (plus E which obviously could not be converted into a three-letter code). ARE was not commenced till July 1934 as at that time RE combinations were used for four-wheeled vehicles and RF was used for motorcycles and more motorcycles were registered than other vehicles! Thus RF was finished before RE. Middlesex, Surrey and Kent soon followed Staffordshire by adopting three letters later in 1932. Inevitably when three-letter registrations were introduced, certain combinations were banned as they spelt potentially offensive words, such as GOD, JEW & SEX.

Private car production ceased during the Second World War and less new registrations were needed. Car ownership, however, grew rapidly after the war and the registration system again had to adapt to accommodate this growth. A logical decision was made to reverse the system, putting the numbers before the letters. Staffordshire was the first authority that needed to issue three-letter registrations and it was also the first authority that needed to issue reversed combinations. The first reversed combination

High Street, Uxbridge
Number Plate GK 6974.
Issued in London, September 1930.

was 1000 E issued in April 1953 - it should be noted that most authorities withheld many low numbered reversed one and two-letter combinations to avoid possible confusion with trade plates. Middlesex followed hard on the heels of Staffordshire by issuing 1000 H

Number plate XB 4463
Issued in London, April 1920.

in June 1953. Many authorities issued their one or two letter codes first as reversed combinations, whereas others started with three-letter reversed combinations. Some started both series at once, generally to avoid the problem of having to fit four-digit numbers onto small rear motorcycle plates.

Ever rapidly increasing vehicle growth meant that, although reversing had effectively doubled the number of combinations available the system was again soon "creaking" and further change was necessary. By the outbreak of the Second World War all available two-letter codes had been allocated except those containing I or Z reserved for Ireland and BF, OO & WC. These latter codes had been withheld for reasons of propriety in the case of BF & WC and in the case of OO because of potential confusion with the figure zero. BF was now allocated to Staffordshire which commenced CBF in July 1960 and OO & WC to Essex who commenced OO in September 1961. The "censors" restricted which combinations of these letters could be issued. Neither BF or WC could be issued as two letter combinations. Similarly ABF, BBF, UBF, AWC & UWC were banned, though following a DVLA review of withheld marks, UBF has recently been issued with "P" prefix. Interestingly, no objections were raised to LOO and POO being issued!

On to year letters

The allocation of BF to Staffordshire and OO & WC to Essex, kept the registration system going temporarily, but a further more radical change was needed. This occurred in 1963 when year letter suffixes were introduced, i.e. the format became ABC 123A.

Staffordshire had been the first authority to use three-letter combinations and the first to issue reversed combinations. The allocation of BF to it, however, "kept it going" and meant that it was not the first authority to run out of available combinations. It was therefore Middlesex who was the first authority to use year letters, AHX 1A being issued in February 1963. Between then and 1 January 1965 all local authorities started using year letters. The reason for this phased introduction was number plate manufacturers wanted time to produce sufficient letters to be able to produce plates. Some authorities were "forced" to go onto year letters as they had run out of forward and reversed combinations. Others did it rather than commence reversed combinations. Yet others did it at an arbitrary point. It is interesting to note that, although Middlesex and other authorities had "run out" of "yearless" combinations, in 1963 some small Scottish authorities were still issuing original format two-letter registrations! The slowest issuing authority, Bute, only reached SJ 2860 before going on to year letters on 1 January 1964!

The allocation of BF, OO & WC in the early 1960's meant that there were now no spare marks for any new county boroughs that might be created. All the Xx codes had been allocated to London except XG (Teeside), XJ (Manchester) & XS (Paisley) (plus Northern Ireland's XI & XZ). When year letters were introduced in 1963 the London Xx codes were withdrawn so spare marks would potentially be available for any new boroughs created. The following were subsequently used: XA - Kircaldy (1963), XB - Coatbridge (1964), XC - Solihull (1964), XD & XE - Luton (1964) & XF - Torbay (1968). When codes were again reallocated in 1974 (we will deal with shortly), all Xx combinations were withdrawn.

Year letters caused a high demand for registration of new vehicles on 1 January each year and this created problems for the motor trade and registration authorities. To minimise the problems that resulted, the "E" letter was used from only 1 January to 31 July 1967 and "F" was commenced on 1 August 1967. 1 August was to remain the changeover date for the next 30 years.

The introduction of year letters with their seven-digit registrations resulted in one change in the appearance of plates. Characters were now 3.7" high, whereas previously they had been 3.1" high. In January 1968 there was a further change to the appearance of plates. Reflective plates, white at the front, black at the rear, were made optional. From 1 January 1972 they became compulsory for most categories of newly registered vehicles.

An indiscernible major change

The changes so far described have for the most part been the result of needing to accommodate increased vehicle ownership. In 1974, what is arguably the most major change of the registration system occurred, but this was not the direct result of the need to "enlarge" the system to cope with more vehicles. Furthermore, the changes would have been totally unnoticeable to the casual observer.

Since the inception of the British system in 1903 all vehicle records had been held in manual form. The records were kept by the authority in which the vehicle keeper resided. Thus, if the police or other official body needed to trace a vehicle's details, they would contact the local authority whose code letters appeared on the plate. Thus, if details of say, ABC 123 were required, Leicester would be contacted as BC denoted Leicester. In many cases, however, the records would no longer be held with the original authority, so the enquiry would be referred on to another local authority in which the keeper now resided. This clearly was not very efficient. Computers had developed to a point where a central computer record could be kept. The decision was made to have a central office at Swansea, the Driver and Vehicle Licensing Centre, with regional offices, Local Vehicle Licensing Offices (LVLO's - now called Local Offices or LO's), responsible for registration of new vehicles.

As with many new computer systems, delays occurred in the introduction of this one. The original plan was that the new system should be introduced on 1 January 1974, during the "M" year. So that local authority and LVLO issues could readily be distinguished, at the beginning of the "M" year, local authorities were instructed to issue M-registrations commencing only with letters in the second half of the alphabet, i.e. N to Y. Some authorities, however, managed to break this rule!

As it happened, the new system was not introduced till 1 October 1974, early in the "N" year. As a result of the way local authority issues had progressed, the decision was made that local authority "N" issues could commence with A to F or N to Y and

LVLO issues would be in the range G to M. One corollary of this is that vehicles registered in August or September 1974 are instantly recognisable!

Obviously, it was necessary to reallocate codes under the new system from local authorities to LVLO's. For the most part, codes "moved" to the nearest LVLO or one relatively near. For instance, Chelmsford LVLO "inherited" Essex's and Southend's codes, plus AR from Hertfordshire. Some codes did, however, "leap across the country". In particular, Scotland was considered to be over-provided with codes, so many Scottish codes "came south". Until 1974, any code containing "S" was automatically recognisable as a Scottish code, but GS was then moved from Perthshire to Luton and WS from Edinburgh to Bristol.

Originally, there were 81 LVLO's. In 1980 (the "W" year), however, following a report from a commission headed by Lord Rayner, the then chairman of Marks and Spencer, 29 LVLO's were closed as an economy measure. In most cases when an office has been closed, a nearby one has taken over responsibility for the issue of the marks from the closed office. Practice in this respect has varied, some such local marks being used much more widely used than others. Since the 1980 round of closures a further 11 offices have been closed, so now 41 LO's remain.

On to year prefixes

"Z" and also, I, O, Q & U were not used as year letters, so the year suffix system expired at the end of the "Y" year, on 31 July 1983. A while beforehand the government had published a consultation paper on what form the system should take after that date and the outcome of this consultation exercise was that the format should be "reversed", i.e. the year letter became a prefix as in A123 ABC.

At the same time a number of other changes were made to the system. Until August 1984, a vehicle which was newly registered second-hand, e.g. because it was imported after being used abroad or was an ex-military vehicle, would receive the current year letter. This meant that some old vehicles had incongruous modern registrations. Furthermore, occasionally people buying second-hand vehicles might be misled regarding its age and some businesses actually imported used vehicles from Ireland or the Channel Islands, so they could profit from them having the latest registration. From 1 August 1984 the government decided that second-hand vehicles newly registered would be given a year letter appropriate to their age. This raised the

problem that it was not always possible to determine the date of a vehicle, e.g. a kit car or a vehicle imported from abroad with inadequate documentation. Such vehicles were therefore to be given a Q-registration, a plate in the format Q123 ABC.

The introduction of year letters made cherished numbers more popular. The decision was therefore made to start A-registration issues at 21 instead of 1, so the numbers A1 to A20 were withheld. Part way through the G-year, the range of numbers withheld was increased to include other "nice" numbers like 30, 33, 100 and 111 and certain car model numbers, such as 911. Subsequently the "Select" Scheme whereby most withheld numbers could be purchased was introduced.

Since registrations were computerised in 1974, most numbers have been allocated to garages in blocks. The garage allocates the numbers to particular vehicles as they are sold, returning to the LO to complete the necessary "paperwork" (or more precisely "computerwork") and obtaining the tax disc before the vehicle is delivered. A few vehicles would be registered directly at the LO, e.g. personal imports, but these would be the exception. A new scheme has, however, now been introduced called Automatic First Registration and Licensing (AFRL). This was first trialled by Ford dealers in Bristol. M-GAE being the first AFRL series. Under this scheme the vehicle is registered by the garage using computer links and the tax disc is issued by the garage. Since P-registration the AFRL scheme has been more widespread.

A consequence of AFRL is that two parallel series have to be used at once, a series for ordinary issues and a series for AFRL. As a result, since the "R" year, registration issues have appeared in a much more random way. Previously they followed a generally logical sequence alphabetically (with the occasional deviation which added interest to my hobby!), but now the progression is much less logical.

The year letter system has increasingly caused problems of a peak of registration in August with around a quarter of new vehicles being registered in that month. This has resulted in pressure from the motor trade for a change in the system and following a consultation exercise a new one was adopted. As a consequence, "R" was used for 13 months, till 31 August 1998 and since then prefix letters have changed every six months, on 1 March and 1 September. This meant that the system lasted till 31 August 2001 when the new system described elsewhere in this book was adopted.

****

The Brighton Run goes past Big Ben, London. A very English setting, but note the Irish number plate. Issued in Armagh, December 1903.

CHAPTER 36.

An Act to amend the Locomotives on Highways Act, 1896. A.D. 1903.
[14th August 1903.]

BE it enacted by the King's most Excellent Majesty, by and with the advice and consent of the Lords Spiritual and Temporal, and Commons, in this present Parliament assembled, and by the authority of the same, as follows :—

1.—(1) If any person drives a motor car on a public highway recklessly or negligently, or at a speed or in a manner which is dangerous to the public, having regard to all the circumstances of the case, including the nature, condition, and use of the highway, and to the amount of traffic which actually is at the time, or which might reasonably be expected to be, on the highway, that person shall be guilty of an offence under this Act. *Reckless driving.*

(2) Any police constable may apprehend without warrant the driver of any car who commits an offence under this section within his view, if he refuses to give his name and address or produce his licence on demand, or if the motor car does not bear the mark or marks of identification.

(3) If the driver of any car who commits an offence under this section refuses to give his name or address, or gives a false name or address, he shall be guilty of an offence under this Act, and it shall be the duty of the owner of the car, if required, to give any information which it is within his power to give, and which may lead to the identification and apprehension of the driver, and if the owner fails to do so he also shall be guilty of an offence under this Act.

2.—(1) Every motor car shall be registered with the council of a county or county borough, and every such council shall assign a separate number to every car registered with them. *Registration of motor cars.*

(2) A mark indicating the registered number of the car and the council with which the car is registered shall be fixed on the car or on a vehicle drawn by the car, or on both, in such manner as the council require in conformity with regulations of the Local Government Board made under this Act.

Extracts from *The Autocar*, *The Times* and *The Car Illustrated,* give a flavour of what was being said at the time of the introduction of the new car registration system.

THE AUTOCAR

A Journal published in the interests of the mechanically propelled road carriage.

EDITED BY H. WALTER STANER.

No. 423.] Vol. XI. Saturday, November 28th, 1903 [Price 3d.

Notes.

The Size of the Numbers.

When the new Motor Car Act, which comes into force on January 1st next, was passed, many points of vital concern were left to the Local Government Board to deal with by means of regulations which they were empowered to make. We need hardly say that the chief features of the Act were the increase of the speed limit from twelve to twenty miles an hour, the imposition of registered numbers, and licenses for driving. In another column to-day we publish a synopsis of the regulations, and it will be seen that the size of the district index letters and the numbers has been very considerably reduced from those originally proposed. Not only so, but the one or two index letters and the car number can be placed in a row if desired, so that a long narrow plate may be employed instead of one more nearly square. This will be a great convenience in many instances, particularly for the front number. Only the back number need be illuminated at night, and so long as it is plainly illuminated, it is left to the automobilist to adopt such means as he sees fit to secure that end. The regulations now issued deal only with the registration, numbering and the driving licences, though in the memorandum which accompanies them, sent to County and County Borough Councils, in which the Act and regulations are expounded for the benefit of those who will administer them, other matters are referred to.

Under the Light Locomotives Act of 1896 certain general regulations as to the use and construction of light locomotives, and the conditions under which they may be used were issued on the 9th day of November, 1896. The Local Government Board now state that, as the result of the passing of the Motor Car Act, 1903, and of the experience gained since 1896, some of the regulations contained in the Order of November 9th, 1896, need amendment; and , in consequence, the Local Government Board will issue an order rescinding these and prescribe others.

It may be mentioned that the term motor cycle is not defined in the Act, and the Local Government Board have no authority to define it, but they understand that, though the term might sometimes properly apply to other vehicles, it would be generally treated as limited to motor cars designed to travel on not more than three wheels, and weighing, unladen, not more than three hundredweights.

The Board contemplate that Councils will usually assign consecutive numbers to cars registered with them. They think, however, that for purposes of ready identification it is not desirable that numbers consisting of more than three figures should be assigned, and they will be prepared, if desired, to assign a fresh index mark to any Council who may require to start a fresh series of numbers under a new mark.

The (Licensing and Registration) Order now issued consists of twenty-two articles, and they are considerably modified from the draft of the Order which the Local Government Board recently sent out to certain of the automobile associations.
The important point about the regulations is that motor cars must carry a number "for and aft", to use a nautical phrase. Only the number carried at the rear of the car requires lighting at night.

DO NOT WORRY

ABOUT THE NEW REGULATION.

You need only apply for your number,

DUNHILLS DO THE REST.

FOR MOTOR CYCLES.

FOR MOTOR CARS.

WILLINGS' ENAMELLED IRON NUMBER PLATES.

Alfred Dunhill. Ltd.. having secured the Sole Agency for these well-known Enamelled Plates. are in a position to make and deliver Regulation Number Plates in four days. These plates are made exactly to meet the requirements of the New Regulation by a special process of enamelling which is unique. inasmuch as it will not scratch with constant cleaning. and is practically everlasting. Price **3/6.**

NEW REGULATION REAR LAMP.

Answering a double purpose—shows a Red Light behind and illuminates the Registration Number. This lamp burns ordinary paraffin : it is fitted with a burner of peculiar construction which causes it to give a clear steady flame. Can be fixed to the ordinary bracket. Strongly made in Brass. price **21/-** : Nickel. price **25/-**

ALFRED DUNHILL, LIMITED,

No. 2. Conduit Street. Regent Street. W.

Telephone 1759 GERRARD.

Head Depot & Wholesale Dept.: 145-7. Euston Rd.. London.

Telephone 35: KING'S CROSS.

Telegrams : "DUNSEND, LONDON."

Number plate advert from 'The Car' dated 30 December 1903.

MOTOR CAR REGULATIONS

———————◆———————

The Highways Committee of the London County Council, to whom the question of dealing with the Motor–Car Act 1903, was delegated by the Council, report that the Local Government Board has now issued its regulations under the Act, together with a circular letter explaining them, and state that they have given careful consideration to the course to be adopted with regard to the administration of the Act.

The regulations prescribe the forms which are to be adopted in connexion with the registration of motor–cars, and the licensing of drivers, and the committee have arranged for the necessary books and forms to be prepared at once, in order that there may be no delay in carrying out the provisions of the Act, which comes into force on January 1 next. The fees prescribed by the Act to be charged for registration are — for a motor–car £1, for a motor–cycle 5s., and the fee for a licence to drive either a motor–car or a motor–cycle is 5s. The Board's regulations prescribe the following as the fees to be charged under section 7 (2) of the Motor-Car Act for the registration of change of ownership of a motor-car or cycle - namely, 5s. in the case of a motor-car, and 1s. in the case of a motor–cycle. The Council is also empowered to charge a fee of 1s. upon the issue of a new driver's licence in place of one lost or defaced. Under section 2 of the Act the Council is empowered, on payment of each annual fee not exceeding £3 as it may decide upon, to assign to a manufacturer or dealer whose business premises are situated in the county a general identification mark which may be used for any car on trial after completion or on trial by an intending purchaser. The committee express the opinion that in this case the *maximum* fee of £3 should be charged, and ask the Council generally to endorse that opinion by resolution.

The Act of 1903 requires that every motor–car shall be registered by the Council and have a separate number assigned to it, while a mark is to be affixed to each car with a view to facilitating identification. The Local Government Board regulations require that two indentification marks, one in front and one behind the car, shall be carried, and for motor–cars two different forms of rectangular plates may be used.

It is provided, moreover, that plates need not be used, but that, should it be preferred, owners may employ designs, painted or other, subject to the requirements of the regulations in respect of the dimensions of the lettering, the colouring,&c., being complied with. Two identification marks have to be carried on motor–cycles, and, provided that the machines do not exceed 3cwt. in weight, various forms of identification plates may be used, and there is some latitude in regard to the position in which they may be carried, while the dimensions, where the vehicles do not exceed this weight, are to be half of those prescribed in the case of motor–cars. The Council may, if it thinks fit, supply to the owner of a car or cycle, should he so desire, the necessary identification plates, but the committee are of opinion that, in view of the various forms of identification marks permitted by the regulations, and also having regard to the fact that, although the registration numbers of motor–cars and cycles are to be consecutive, an entirely different form and size of plate is permitted in the two cases, it would be very undesirable, for the present at any rate, for the Council to supply the plates.

The Board in its regulations and in the circular accompanying them has dealt with the questions arising out of the registration of cars and cycles and the licensing of drivers, these being the most pressing points to be settled. There are certain other matters, however, arising under the Act of 1903 which will have to receive attention at a later date, when a better opportunity shall have been afforded the Council of judging of the effect of the provisions of the Act upon motor–car traffic. The matters to which the committee here refer are dealt with particularly by sections 8, 9 and 10 of the Act relative to (1) the prohibition of motor–cars on special roads; (2) the limitation of the rate of speed; and (3) the erection of notice boards. With regard to the question of the limitation of speed, the committee point out that the Local Government Board is of opinion that the expedients provided by the Act for the reduction of the speed limit in certain districts to ten miles an hour, and for the prohibition of the use of motor vehicles in certain streets, should not be resorted to, unless it is seen that the other provisions of the Act make such a course indispensable. Having carefully considered this point, the committee state that they fully concur in the views expressed by the Board.

For the information and guidance of the public, the committee have arranged for the issue of an advertisement stating the date by which the Council will be prepared to register motor–cars and motor–cycles and to issue licences for drivers, and stating further that, owing to the various forms of identification marks allowed by the Board's regulations, the Council will not provide plates for use of owners. They state that they propose to submit, after the Council shall have had an opportunity of judging of the working of the Act, a further report, if necessary, dealing in detail with the various matters arising thereunder. It is, however, necessary for the Council at once to decide what fee shall be charged for the assignment of a general identification mark to a manufacturer or dealer, and, as already stated, they are of opinion that this should be the *maximum* allowed by the Act. They add that the solicitor did not consider it necessary for drivers' licences to be issued under the seal of the Council, a course which would entail serious delay and inconvenience and they have accordingly arranged for these to be issued by the clerk of the Council.

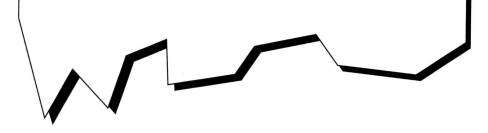

THE TIMES 1ST JANUARY, 1904

MOTOR–CARS

The Locomotives on Highways Act, 1896, defines a "light
locomotive" as : —
"Any vehicle propelled by mechanical power if it is under three tons
in weight unladen, and is not used for the purpose of drawing more
than one vehicle (such vehicle with its locomotive not to exceed in
weight unladen four tons) and is so constructed that no smoke or
visible vapour is emitted therefrom except from any temporary or
accidental cause."
The Motor-Car Act [U.K.], which comes into operation to-day, and
is limited to expire on December 31, 1906, gives to "motor-car" the
same meaning as that of "fight locomotive" in the above enactment,
except that (1) for the purpose of new registration provisions
"motor–car" is not to include a vehicle drawn by a motor-car, and
(2) the weights mentioned therein may be increased as respects any
class of vehicle by Local Government Board regulations.
The reckless, negligent, or too rapid driving (at what-ever speed) on
a public highway or roadway to which the public are granted access
is an offence under the Act, and any police-constable may apprehend
without warrant a driver who has offended within his view if he
refuses to give his name and address or produce the licence required
by the Act, or if the car cannot be identified under the Act. Every car
must be registered with the council of a county or county borough
with a separate number and mark indicating it fixed on the car or
vehicle drawn by it or both, and on payment of a fee of 5s. each for
motor–cycles and 20s. each for other cars. Manufacturers and
dealers may obtain general identification marks for use on trial. As
to licences, it is enacted that:–
"A person shall not drive a motor–car on a public highway (or
roadway to which the public are granted access) unless he is licensed
for that purpose, and a person shall not employ any person who is
not so licensed to drive a motor–car.
"The council of a county or county borough shall grant a license to
drive a motor–car to any person applying for it who resides in that
county or county borough on payment of a fee of 5s., unless the
applicant is disqualified under the provisions of this Act."
The only absolute disqualifications are – (1) being under 17 years of
age, for driving motor cycles only, of 14 years or under; and (2)
already holding a licence still in force. But a person convicted of an
offence under the Act or of any offence in connexion with the
driving of a motor–car (other than a first or second offence
consisting solely of exceeding any limit of speed fixed under
the Act) may be declared to be disqualified by the Court before
whom (sic) he is convicted for a period limited only by the

70

Regtransfers.co.uk

discretion of that Court. The fine for any offence under the Act may be up to £20, or in the case of a second or subsequent conviction up to £50, with the alternative of imprisonment up to three months, but there will be an appeal to quarter sessions against (1) imprisonment, (2) any fine above 20s., and (3) any order of disqualification. The enforcement of the *maximum* speed of 14 miles an hour under the Act of 1896 (as reduced by Local Government Board regulations under that Act to 12 miles an hour) is replaced by the enactment that: —

"A person shall not, under any circumstances, drive a motor car on a public highway or roadway to which the public are granted access at a speed exceeding 20 miles an hour, and within any limits or place referred to in regulations made by the Local Government Board with a view to the safety of the public, on the application of the local authority of the area in which the limits or place are situate, a person shall not drive a motor-car at a speed exceeding 10 miles an hour." Contravention of this enactment is punishable by fine up to £10 for a first offence, £20 for a second, and £50 for any subsequent offence; but there can be no conviction merely on the opinion of one witness, nor unless the offender was warned of an intended prosecution at the time of the offence, or unless notice of it was sent to him or to the registered owner of the car within reasonable time after the commission of it. The Local Government Board may also prohibit or restrict the driving of any motor-car on any highway which does not exceed 16 feet in width "or on which ordinary motor-car traffic would in their opinion be especially dangerous." Local authorities are to give public notice of any such prohibitions or restrictions or limitations of speed, and also, subject to regulation as to size and colour" to be made by the Board, to set up sign-posts denoting dangerous corners, cross-roads, and precipitous places. In case of accident to any person or to a horse or vehicle in charge of any person owing to the presence of a motor-car on a road, the driver is directed to stop and give his and the owner's name, if required, on pain of a fine up to £10 for a first offence, £20 for a second, and £20 or imprisonment up to one month for any subsequent offence. All common law and statutory liabilities of owners are expressly left unaffected– a very extensive saving, in view of the wide civil liability for negligence and of the direction of the Act of 1896 that a motor–car, or "light locomotive" as it is there called, is to be deemed a "carriage" within the meaning of any Act whatever – and both the Act of 1896 and the new Act are declared to apply to persons in the public service of the Crown.

Margate Fishing Festival 1913
Number plate LA 6653

THE TIMES WEDNESDAY, JANUARY 13, 1904

THE MOTOR–CAR ACT.

Mr. Marsham, sitting at Bow-Street, had before him the first case under the Motor-Car Act, 1903. HENRY SMITH, described as a motor-car driver, of Coliseum-terrace, Regent's-Park, was charged with being drunk while in charge of a motor–car, and with failing to produce his driver's licence when requested to do so by a police-officer. The second offence was framed under the Motor–car Act, 1903, sec. 3, subsec. 4. A police-constable said that at 8 o'clock yesterday morning he saw the prisoner, who was drunk, driving two gentlemen, also under the influence of drink, in a motor-car in Bedford-street. He was going at a slow pace, but was wandering from one side of the road to the other. When asked for his licence he said he had left it at home. The prisoner said he was not aware that he had to produce his licence whenever it was demanded by a police-officer. As to the charge of drunkenness, he said he was more tired than drunk; he had been driving all night. Mr. Marsham dealt with the prisoner under the first subsection of the Act for driving a motor-car in a negligent or reckless manner. The offence was a serious one and was punishable with a £20 penalty, but, this being the first time the prisoner had been charged he would only fine him £10. For the second offence the *maximum* fine was £5, but as the Act had only just come into operation he would impose the mitigated penalty of 5s. He would, however, deal more severely with similar cases in the future.

Superstition as to the ill luck attaching to the number 13 has made itself apparent. A Shropshire journal reports that in that county this number fell in the ordinary course to a lady motorist. She promptly had it sent back and said she would prefer a change. The request was acceded to. This, however, was not the end of the difficulty. A driver sent to register his master's car accepted the discarded No. 13 but came back next day with the message that his master's daughter would be better satisfied with another number! "Thirteen" after this was not tried again with cars and it is now cancelled so far as the county of Salop is concerned.

The Motor Car Journal, 9.1.04.

War Department vehicles handed over to Slough Trading Company – cancellation of registration numbers. All War Department vehicles disposed of through the Slough Trading Company should be regarded as not having been previously registered, (even if by accident numbers remain on the vehicles).....
In cases where the registration marks and numbers have not been removed from vehicles prior to their arrival at the Slough Trading Company's deport, the Company will take steps to delete the registration marks and numbers...

Circular RF 155 4.8.22.

The attention of the Ministry has been drawn to the fact that some Registration Authorities require that a person allotted an identification number of less than four figures shall, on the identification plates, prefix noughts so as to make four figures. In view of the Minister's proposals in connection with general identification marks, (details of which will be communicated later), it is requested that this practice may be discontinued in future cases. It is also understood that some Registration Authorities duplicate the identification numbers, e.g. the same number may be allotted both to a motor car and to a motor cycle. Under the new scheme such duplication may entail confusion and I am to ask that it may be discontinued in all future cases."

Circular RF 105 29.11.20

Editorial Jottings.

THE REGISTRATIONS.

In anticipation of the coming into operation of the new Act on January 1st, large numbers of automobilists have already registered their cars or motor cycles, particularly in the metropolitan district.

There has been some amount of competition for the securing of the number plate "A 1" and this has been acquired by Earl Russell for his Napier car.

From other centres we hear that registration has been proceeding busily, automobilists recognising that the earlier their application the better their chance of obtaining a small number. Inasmuch as the size of the number-plate is not arbitrary, but has only to have a specified margin in addition to the actual letters and figures, it follows that the recipient of a single figure has a smaller plate than a man who is allotted a two-figure mark, and he in his turn is more fortunate than the later applicant who receives three figures as his official number.

In Liverpool, on the first day for the registration of cars, writes our local correspondent, there was quite a rush of owners of private machines to secure a single letter number. In less than five minutes after the opening of the municipal buildings at nine o' clock, all the units were taken up, No. 1 on the register being secured by Mr. A. G. Lyster, engineer to the Mersey Docks and Harbour Board.

There is one point however, in the
All Cars, whether regulations which I think is an alteration for
Slow or Fast, the worse. In the previous draft, vehicles
Numbered. which did not exceed a maximum speed of
twelve miles per hour were exempted from
carrying big numbers, and were allowed to carry alternative
plates one-sixth the size of the ordinary number plates. This
clause has now been eliminated, and the electric brougham, for
example, which in most cases is not capable of a speed of more
than fifteen miles per hour, if that, and is used solely as a town
carriage, must now carry numbers as big as the fastest racing car.
The object of identification is to catch those cars which cannot
be overtaken under ordinary circumstances, and which are likely
to go some distance before they can be traced. It is therefore
difficult to see why cars incapable of a speed in excess of twelve
miles per hour or so should be thus penalised in the same way as
the faster vehicles, or, in fact, more than horse vehicles.

Most of the county councils appear at present to
Illegal Number- be placing the onus on the individual
plates. automobilist of satisfying the legal requirements
as to the form and size of his number-plate, and
are not demanding that the latter shall be submitted for official
inspection before being affixed to the car. Several cars have been
seen about London, however, during the last few days with
plates which by no means conform to the official requirements,
and one four-figured plate which was remarked in Piccadilly was
barely the size of one containing two figures only of the correct
dimensions. It is to be hoped that this sort of thing may not
become observable to any appreciable degree, otherwise the
county councils may perforce indulge in domiciliary visits, or
instruct the police to prosecute more or less tiresome
researches with a view to determine whether number-plates
generally are affixed in proper form.

"A 1."

In most of the counties the coveted figure "1" has been secured by a member of the council. London is no exception to the rule, and "A 1" is the property of Earl Russell, L.C.C. We are surprised to note, however, in the photograph

EARL RUSSELL'S "A I" CAR

from which the accompanying illustration was made, that the number-plate of so astute a person as Earl Russell should not be *en règle*. It will be seen that the dash which should appear between the index letter and the figure of a horizontal plate is missing on Earl Russell's car.

Earl Russell's Number-Plate

Sir. —Referring to the photograph of my car, your critic is mistaken in saying that my number plate is not *en règle*. I have only been "astute" enough to read the regulations, and I do not anywhere find that the dash between the letter and the figure is prescribed. To insert this dash would be to put upon the plate something contrary to the regulations.

I think I noticed in a previous issue that you commented unfavourably on the refusal of the L.C.C. to start a new index letter after the first thousand. As I was responsible for this, I would point out to your critic what he has apparently overlooked, that four figures and one letter do not take up more room than three figures and two letters. As there are no more single letters available, a new index letter will have to consist of two letters, and you will probably agree that the L.C.C. were studying the interests of automobilists in the course they took.

—I am sir, your obedient servant.

RUSSELL.

Telegraph House, Chichester.

Earl Russell's Number-plate.

According to the defence urged by Earl Russell on behalf of the form of number-plate which he has adopted, and which was illustrated in the last issue of The Car, the omission of the hyphen between the letter A and the figure I was intentional on his part. He contends, in short, that it is the hyphen and not its absence that is illegal. It is perfectly true that the Local Government Board regulations did not specifically define, in so many words, that the hyphen shall be used in the case of the horizontal number-plates: but, as everyone knows by now, the hyphen is clearly marked in the illustrations printed with the order, and it is further stated that "the mark and number must be arranged in conformity with the arrangements of figures issued in one or other of the alternative diagrams." It is further stated that whereas, in the alternative diagram No. 1, in which the letters are above the figures, the space between the upper and lower lines must be three quarters of an inch, in the alternative diagram No.2 where the letters and figures are on the same line.

EARL RUSSELL'S NUMBER-PLATE

SIR.— I notice that you admit in a somewhat ungracious paragraph that you were wrong as to the hyphen on my number-plate. I urged no defence ; I simply pointed out that your comment was inaccurate. It is not perhaps wonderful that you fail to understand the regulations, since you cannot even quote them correctly. You say in your quotation "the mark and number must be arranged in conformity with the *arrangements of figures issued in* one or other of the alternative diagrams." The actual words of the order are "the mark and number being arranged in conformity with the *arrangements of letters and figures shown on* one or other of the alternative diagrams." The hyphen is neither a figure nor a letter.

Since I have already stated my reason for omitting the hyphen your statement that this "course suggests an unprofitable desire to take advantage of an accidental lack of definition" should not have been made. It is quite sufficient to have displayed your ignorance without being discourteous to a correspondent who corrects you.— I am, Sir, your obedient servant.

Grays Inn.   RUSSELL.

[So far as the misquotation is concerned, we may explain that this was merely a typist's error, and one, moreover, which certainly did not affect the argument to our advantage. As to a hyphen not being a figure, the claim put forward by Lord Russell is, to say the least, novel: the meaning of the word "figure" is by no means invariably confined to the sense of "numeral." Our reference to the "unprofitable desire" had a general, not a personal, application, for we had already encountered several automobilists who hailed with satisfaction the "lack of definition" to which THE CAR referred, and were prepared to take advantage thereof. In Ireland the absence of a hyphen after the letter "I" would cause obvious confusion, as may be seen by reference to the illustration on page 345 of the present issue, in which a car numbered "AI-15" would be read as "AI15" if the hyphen were deleted. Action of this kind would only result in the imposition of more stringent restrictions, and for this reason we contended, and reiterate the contention, that such a course is unprofitable.—ED.]

Earl Russell's Number-Plate.

Sir. — Although it is quite true, as contended by Earl Russell, that there is nothing in the wording of the Local Government Board Regulations to require a dash to be inserted between the letters and figures on a single line number-plate, may I point out that the Fourth Schedule includes two alternative diagrams, and the first clause of the "Provisions to be compiled with" says "...the mark and number being arranged in conformity with the arrangement of letters and figures shown on one or other of the alternative diagrams." It seems to me that although the word "dash" is not mentioned, the "arrangement of letters and figures shown "includes the arrangement of letters divided by a dash from the figures, so that Earl Russell's contention seems to be incorrect. — Yours faithfully.

A.J.Wilson.

Illegal Number-plates.

A less serious matter, perhaps, but one which further illustrates this curious tendency to do the wrong thing, is that which concerns the non-observance of the various regulations in the Registration and Use and Construction Orders of the Local Government Board. Hardly a day passes but what we see cars with number-plates which are in no sense in conformity with official requirements. The numbers are of the wrong size, and are not separated by the correct distances from each other or the distinguishing letter which precedes them. In some cases, of course, the variations are trivial, but not universally so by any means. And where is the excuse? At the time the new regulations were promulgated they were printed in every automobile journal, while newcomers in the field have every opportunity of ascertaining what is the correct thing to do: hence excuse there is none. There are other regulations which are ignored, and we only refrain from specifying these because the police in certain districts are but too ready to seize upon every technical breach, and carry the enforcement of the letter of the law to the degree of undiscriminating persecution.

CORRESPONDENCE.

A WARNING TO MOTOR-CAR DEALERS.

SIR. — A friend of mine has been summoned under the new Act for driving a 16 h.p. car "without the said car being registered." The circumstances are as follows:– He and I drove in the car to a certain police court on the 5th inst. I got out to ask a constable where we might leave the car whilst we were in the court, when a police inspector came up and ordered his man to take the number off the car. On my asking why, he replied that it was not on test or taking out a prospective customer. Now, I have paid the L.C.C. £3 for a Dealer's General Identification Mark, and the necessary two number plates were affixed to the car in the proper positions. I understand that the purpose of registration and identification plates is to enable the authorities to put their hands on anyone who breaks the law - to identify in fact - but if one is to be hauled up for taking a car out under such circumstances it seems to me that the law becomes a farce, and one is liable to be held up at any time.

If a conviction follows in this case it means that all sorts of possibilities open out. For instance, if I want to give a run to a man I should be liable to be stopped whilst driving to his house or returning. I might want to go and see a client on a matter of detail, but apparently I must not take a car out for such a purpose. I think, from enquiries made, that dealers do not know how this matter stands, so it might be well if you could take it up in your paper in the interests of the trade. I enclose, for your information, copy of the letter I wrote to the L.C.C., also copy of their reply. They do not answer my question, but surely the certificate is clear proof of registration. Yours faithfully.

A MOTOR-CAR DEALER.

No. 104, MAY 18, 1904

THE CAR

Straining the Law.

Several new points have lately arisen in connection with the Motor Car Act of 1903, not the least important of which is referred to in a letter we print this week from "A Motor–car Dealer." Parliament has made special provision for dealers' marks, on the assumption that they will be used by persons who are in the trade for the purpose of trading. It now appears that the wording of the Act has been strained in the direction of preventing any general inclusion under this heading. I intend to ask a question in the House of Commons shortly on this point
– in fact before this appears in print I may have had an opportunity of doing so. Another important oversight seems to me that a bench of magistrates appears to have no option in the matter of endorsement of licences if a motorist is convicted under Section I of the Act. The word, of course, should have been "may" instead of "shall," for I am sure that neither the President of the Local Government Board nor Parliament ever intended to compel a bench of magistrates to endorse a man's licence when the offence was of a trivial nature. Obviously, this power was only intended to be used in cases where a driver had been proved guilty of driving to the actual and real danger of the public.

No. 189, JANUARY 3, 1906

THE CAR

Numbers and Obscuration.

Some prosecutions have taken place lately for obscuration of numbers such as will inevitably arise sometimes from splashed mud. In a few cases the magistrates have dismissed the charge, but in some a fine has been imposed. A curious case has just occurred in the south of England, where the glass of the lamp which illuminates the back number had become so thickly covered with mud in a long run that it failed to give a sufficient light on the number. The police are considering the matter, which is, in my opinion, undoubtedly a technical breach of the Act, but there are other reasons which may induce the authorities to drop the matter. It is quite clear, however, and quite right also, that a back or front number should be kept readable, or otherwise identification of offenders becomes well nigh impossible.

It may be asked, perhaps, by the unthinking **The Need for** why there need be any distinction between **Trade "Marks."** makers' "marks" and the ordinary number-plates of private owners; in other words, why should not the manufacturer register a car as soon as it is built? The answer is fairly obvious. When an individual car is registered the name and residence of its owner have to be entered on the certificate, as well as the type and colour of the body. If a maker always fitted every *chassis* with a body and then registered the combination, many of his customers would demand a different type and a different colour alike, and the particulars would have to be amended accordingly; while even if a car were taken as it stood the purchaser would still have to notify the county council of the change of ownership, which would mean that an extra 10s. would be received on every car on transference from manufacturer to owner. If, moreover, the customer preferred to register his car in the county where he lived instead of that of the manufacturer, he would have to register it anew and pay a sovereign ere receiving a fresh number-plate. Apart from this matter of the councils profiting twice over upon every car, it would be absurd to treat a firm of manufacturers as a private owner on a colossal scale, and make them pay £1 on every car which they turned out, and which they actually owned for a few minutes only; for, as a rule, the purchaser is only too eager to take delivery as soon as a car has had its coachwork finished after the testing of the *chassis*. But let no one imagine for a moment that a motor-car, in skeleton form or fully equipped and painted, is allowed to be driven on the roads of this country without means of identification. That is a privilege reserved for the King, and, of course, the very fact of the exception declares the identity of the royal car at a glance.

144 MX issued in
Middlesex, August 1917

Mr. A.A. Speechley was given this World War I tank named 'Jenny Jones' by
Ealing Council and used his trade plate 144 MX when he moved it from Dean
Gardens, Uxbridge Road, West Ealing to 'Speechley's Yard', Bath Road,
Longford on Sunday February 12, 1933.

MR. A.A. SPEECHLEY'S ROLLS ROYCE. THURS 20 JUNE
1935

WET ROAD, A SKID, THEN—THIS

HE AND HIS 4 YEARS OLD SON BRIAN SURVIVED.

Six people were injured, four seriously, in this collision at Harold
Wood, on the main Colchester road yesterday. Driver of the car
was not one of them. Wet roads and a bad skid are blamed
for the crash.

Number Plate AK-3747 issued in Bradford, December 1903. Trade plate 723 H,
issued in Middlesex 1912. Are these plates still in circulation?

THE NEW NUMBER-PLATE.

An interesting epoch in the development of automobilism is marked by the fact that 10,000 motor vehicles have now been registered in London. Since our last issue the Local

Number Plate LC-30

LONDON'S NEW NUMBER-PLATE.

Government Board has promulgated an official order to the effect that the letters "LC" have been awarded to the London County Council as a distinguishing mark in lieu of the letter "A" which has hitherto done duty. Clearly this decision was made none too soon, for, as the accompanying illustration shows, the Council has already entered upon its second series. The numbers LC 1 to 29 have been retained by the Council for its Works Department, and the first number issued to an applicant from the general public is LC 30, which is now affixed to the Decauville belonging to Mr. R. Moffatt Ford.

Outline of the Legislation

by Les Newall

Before 1903

As early as 1681 it was required that carts licensed to ply for hire in the City of London should be marked with the City coat of arms and a number on a brass plate. The London Hackney Carriage Act of 1831 referred to "stage coaches.......being duly licensed and having proper numbered plates" and before the end of the century London and probably other local authorities required hackney carriages to carry numbered plates.

The Revenue Act of 1869, effective 1 January 1870, imposed a uniform system of taxation for horse-drawn carriages. The Locomotives Act of 1898 required county councils or county borough councils to register or license "heavy locomotives", (excluding those used for agricultural purposes), operating within their area. A "heavy locomotive" was one with an unladen weight of or exceeding 3 tons, (in practice almost exclusively steam powered vehicles).

The Motor Car Act, 1903

This was the first legislation to require the universal registration of motor vehicles, and the requirement to carry number plates. Section 2 includes the following sub-sections:

(1)   Every motor car shall be registered with the council of a county or county borough, and every such council shall assign a separate number to every car registered with them.

(2)   A mark indicating the registered number of the car and the council with which the car is registered shall be fixed on the car or on a vehicle drawn by the car, or on both, in such manner as the council require in conformity with regulations of the Local Government Board made under this Act.

The Act came into force on 1st January 1904. "Heavy locomotives" were excluded from the registration provisions of the 1903 Act since they were already required to be registered or licensed under the Locomotives Act of 1898. The Heavy Motor Car Order of 1904 redefined the upper weight limit for a "motor car" from 3 tons to 5 tons and thus vehicles with unladen weights between these figures became regulated by the Motor Car Act of 1903 rather than the Locomotives Act of 1898. Tramcars were also excluded from the provisions of the Act.

The Regulations of 1903

The regulations referred to in Section 2 of the 1903 Act duly appeared as:
The Motor Car (Registration & Licensing) Order, 1903. Statutory Rules and Orders 1903, No. 998.
The Motor Car Registration & Licensing (Scotland) Order 1903, SR&O 1903, No. 1001.
The Motor Car (Registration & Licensing) (Ireland) Order 1903, SR&O 1903, No. 1002.

The following is a summary of their main provisions:
Article I of Part I required that "The Council of every County and the Council of every County Borough shall establish and keep a Register (hereinafter referred to as "the Register of Motor Cars") for the registration of motor cars. The index mark distinguishing the Council of the County or County Borough with which a motor car is registered shall...... be the letter or letters shown opposite to the name of that Council in Part I of the First Schedule to this Order". This article required that the register was to be kept in the form specified in the Second Schedule and provided that the Council may, if they thought fit, keep the Register in two parts, one relating to motor cars and the other to motor cycles.

Article II specified the fees for registration and Article III required that the Council, on receipt of an application for registration "shall forthwith assign a separate number to the motor car..."

Article IV provided that on change of ownership "an application shall be made either to cancel the registration of the car or to continue the existing registration under the new ownership."

Article VI stated "If the Council are satisfied that a motor car which has been registered with them is destroyed, broken up, or permanently removed from the United Kingdom, or registered with another registering authority under the Act of 1903, or if the owner of a registered motor car...... requests them to cancel the registration...... they shall cause the entries in the Register of Motor Cars...... to be cancelled and may, if they think fit, assign the registered number of the motor car to any other motor car belonging to the same or any other owner".

Article VII: "The mark to be carried by a registered motor car, in pursuance of section 2 of the Act of 1903, shall consist of two plates which must conform as to lettering, numbering and otherwise, with the provisions set out in the Fourth Schedule to this Order. Designs , painted or otherwise, shown upon the motor car may, if it is desired, be used instead of plates..."

Article VIII Dealt with the positioning of plates, (one front, one rear, in an upright position), and provided for the use of double sided plates on the front of motor cycles or tricycles not exceeding 3 cwt. unladen. Article IX provided for the display of a duplicate plate on a trailer. Article X permitted Councils, if they thought fit, to supply plates and make a charge for them. Article XI provided for the illumination of rear plates during hours of darkness. Article XII dealt with the assignment to manufacturers or dealers of a general identification mark and specified the form such marks should take.

Order of Issue of Index Marks

by Les Newall

One and two letter marks preceding numbers

Although the Act decreed that registration should be in effect from 1 January 1904, most authorities commenced registering vehicles in December 1903 and a few in November. The oft-repeated claim that A 1 was the first British registration is meaningless in this context - thousands of vehicles had already been registered before the operative date. Indeed, the evidence is that A 1 was not allocated until December 1903, (the exact date is not available since all the LCC's records have been destroyed), whilst Buckinghamshire, Somerset and Hastings had commenced registering vehicles in November.

There was usually a time lag between the date of allotment of a mark by a SR&O and the date the mark was taken into use, but one and two-letter index marks were brought into use in the same order in which they were allotted by SR&O, with very few exceptions. The late issue of OC has already been referred to, and the only other case where the order of allocation and the order of issue differed was that of some of the London County Council's later issues.

Three letter marks preceding numbers

Three-letter index marks were not always issued in alphabetical sequence. Staffordshire's first three marks were ARF, (the very first three-letter issue in July 1932), BRF and CRF, because although RF was finished, RE was still in use for motorcycles only. Next after ARF was Middlesex with AMY, issued out of sequence to celebrate Amy Johnson's historic flight. Numerous authorities, (e.g. Bedfordshire, Birkenhead, Coventry and Southampton) issued their three-letter marks in the same order in which their two-letter marks had been allotted, e.g. for Bedfordshire: ABM, ANM, ATM, AMJ - not ABM, AMJ, ANM, and ATM etc. Devon adopted a unique system. They took each two-letter mark in the order in which it had been allotted and issued it in as many three-letter combinations as had been allotted in the latest SR&O. Thus, the initial order was ATA, BTA, ATT, BTT, AUO, BUO, ADV, BDV, AOD, BOD and this pattern continued throughout to YOD. Middlesex allocated certain combinations to major distributors and this led to irregularities in the order of issue but a major departure from the normal order took place in late 1938 when RHX to RMY were specially allotted to the War Department (normal Middlesex issues were then in the Kxx series), followed by PHX to PMY and SHX.

In general, three-letter index marks were used only when the authority in question had exhausted its two-letter series. There were a few exceptions, e.g. Staffordshire, who continued to issue RE for motorcycles until it reached 9999 in 1947 and Middlesex, who still had several incomplete two-letter series when they commenced issuing three-letter marks. Some of the smaller Scottish counties were still using two-letter marks until they commenced the year-letter system in 1964 or 1965.

Reserved series

There are numerous instances of complete series being allotted to a single registrant. Mention has already been made of the fact that complete series were reserved for War Department vehicles by Middlesex, with whom almost all military vehicles had been registered since 1921. In the two-letter era blocks of up to 2000 numbers had been reserved, but with the onset of three-letter marks complete blocks of 999 were set aside, (although in the first few "War Department" series the numbers 1-20 were omitted from the block issue.) Several complete series and large blocks in other series were issued solely to armoured vehicles and when in the post-war years Middlesex were running short of available marks, many of these series and blocks were used again for normal issue. Since the possibility of armoured vehicles transferring to civilian use could be ignored, the usual objections to the reissue of void numbers did not apply.

The largest recipient of complete series was, however, the General Post Office, almost all of whose vehicles were registered by the London County Council until 1 October 1969 when they commenced to be registered locally. Between 1939 and 1969 over 150 complete or near complete blocks were thus reserved. London also reserved complete series for other government departments.

Watford was the home of the L.M.S. Railway's road motor department and Hertfordshire allotted several complete series to the railway company and, later, to the London Midland Region of British Railways. Two cities (Birmingham with JOJ and Glasgow with SGD) reserved whole series for their municipal bus fleet and, in the latter case, other Corporation vehicles.

Another notable recipient of complete blocks was the vehicle distribution company, Stewart and Ardern, who for a long period had their own series issued by Middlesex, usually with separate series for private and commercial vehicles in use simultaneously.

When the Home Delivery Export Scheme commenced in 1953, London, Birmingham and Coventry reserved complete series for these issues.

Complete, or almost complete, series were also allotted to Claude Rye, motorcycle dealer (RYE) and Sir Alfred McAlpine, public works contractors (MCA).

Segregation of vehicle types

A few authorities, notably London, Middlesex and Birmingham registered commercial vehicles and/or motorcycles separately from cars.

Order of Issue of Registration Numbers

by Les Newall

One and two letter marks preceding numbers

1903 to 1920

It was initially envisaged that single and two-letter index marks would be followed by the numbers 1 to 999. The Local Government Board's circular to county and county borough councils dated 20th November 1903, which set out the minutiae of the operation of the Motor Car Act, contained in this paragraph:
"The Board contemplate that Councils will usually assign consecutive numbers to cars registered with them. They think, however, that for purposes of ready identification, it is not desirable that numbers consisting of more than three figures should be assigned, and they will be prepared, if desired, to assign a fresh index mark to any Council who may require to start a fresh series of numbers under a new mark". However, it would appear that the Local Government Board very quickly had second thoughts, even before London exhausted its initial mark, since it must have become obvious that the increasing use of cars would require a system with a greater capacity than originally envisaged. Thus, all one and two-letter marks were followed by up to four numerals.

The commonest method of issue of registration numbers was, of course, to allot numbers sequentially from 1 to 9999, but there were numerous variations from this practice. Article IV of the 1903 Regulations stated "If the ownership of the car is changed, notice of the change shall be given either by the new, or the old owner to the Council with which the motor car is registered, and an application shall also be made either to cancel the registration of the car or to continue the existing registration under the new ownership". Article VI provided that "If the Council are satisfied that a motor car which has been registered with them is destroyed, broken up, permanently removed from the United Kingdom, or registered with another registering authority under the Act of 1903, or if the owner of a registered motor car by application in writing requests them to cancel the registration thereof (except where in the case of a change in ownership, there is an application to continue the existing registration) they shall cause the entries in the Register of Motor Cars with respect to the motor car to be cancelled, and may, if they think fit, assign the registered number of the motor car to any other motor car whether belonging to the same or any other owner." Thus, these two regulations authorised the re-issue of void numbers, and it was possible for a car to receive a new number on change of ownership, or for a new car to receive a void registration number. (The Roads Act of 1920 put an end to this practice). The 1903 Regulations further specified that "The Council of any County or County Borough may, if they think fit, keep the Register of Motor Cars in two parts, one relating to motor cars not being motor cycles, and the other part relating to motorcycles." In those early days motorcycles were, in some areas, as numerous as cars. As with much of the original legislation, there was no uniformity of practice between the various authorities. Many simply kept separate registers for the two categories, but used a common sequence of numbers issued in numerical order as and when required. At the other extreme were those authorities who not only kept separate registers, but also adopted a separate and duplicate sequence of numbers for motorcycles; in many cases the two series continued side by side until the end of 1920. Derbyshire, for example issued to the end of 1920 R 1-5395 for cars and R 1-5795 for cycles; from 1.1.21 a common series R 5796 upwards. (In a few cases there were three parallel series, in the case of those authorities using a separate sequence for Heavy Motor Cars). Other authorities, whilst using a common series of numbers, adopted numbering schemes by means of which motorcycles could readily be identified.

Number Plate BL 2910
Issued in Berkshire, January 1904.

Re-issue of Void Numbers

by Les Newall

The reissue of numbers previously used was frowned upon after 1920 and the only noteworthy exceptions before 1955 were QQ 1000-9999 and the Middlesex blocks originally allocated to armoured vehicles of the War Department.

However, in response to a growing desire for "cherished" numbers, in 1955 the Ministry of Transport instructed local authorities that they could, on request and on payment of the then statutory fee of £5 for a cherished transfer, re-issue a registration mark and number if they were satisfied that the vehicle to which it had been originally issued had either been destroyed or permanently exported.
This concession was discontinued in 1962.

Thereafter the reissue of used numbers was confirmed to the special marks for heads of diplomatic missions and to veteran and vintage vehicles of genuine historic interest; Bournemouth was prominent in reissuing a number of EL's for this purpose, especially in the EL 1xxx range. This practice ceased with the introduction of "Age-Related" marks in 1983.

It has been suggested by several Registration Authorities that in order to avoid the allotment of additional Index Marks, the proper course is for them to search the old registers, cancel registrations which appear to be dead, and reissue the numbers.
The Minister, however, is not in favour of the adoption of this procedure - at any rate, for the present."   Circular RF 150, 2.3.22

The arrangement for the issue of void marks was discontinued by the Minister in 1962. No void mark should therefore be reissued by a Council unless they are expressly authorised to do so by the Driving and Motor Licences Division of the Ministry to certain exceptional circumstances.

A reconditioned vehicle of this kind, (i.e. a "Veteran" car), would, of course be entitled to keep the original registration mark if it had been registered under the Motor Car Act of 1903, but where it is impossible to produce evidence to this effect or the vehicle is a "rebuild" it is allotted a registration mark from the current series. In view of the special Construction & Use arrangements it has been agreed that it would be desirable to allocate an index mark more appropriate to the vehicle's age. Councils are asked, therefore, to give sympathetic consideration to any requests for appropriate numbers for these vehicles. Because of the ban on the reissue of void marks imposed by the Minister in 1962 it will be desirable to refer any case to this Department where it is not possible to meet such a request from unused marks in an earlier series. Consideration will then be given to the reissue of a "void" mark to meet the exceptional circumstances. It cannot be too strongly emphasised that this should not be regarded as a relaxation of the ban on the reissue of "void" marks. Only a very small number of vehicles should fail to be dealt with under the foregoing paragraph.

M.o.T. "Handbook", 1965 edition.

****

International Circulation

by Les Newall

The U.K. was party to the International Convention on Motor Traffic of 11 October 1909 and under the Provisional Regulations of 9 March 1921 the special mark QQ was allotted for issue to vehicles arriving in this country without a valid International Travelling Pass issued under the Convention. The principal motoring organisations were appointed as registration authorities for the purpose of these temporary registrations and, although all 'Q' combinations were normally allotted to the London County Council, (and subsequently to the Greater London Council and London Central VRO), by far the greater number of 'Q' registrations are, in fact, allocated through the Automobile Association and the Royal Automobile Club. Initially QQ 1-1000 were allotted to the County Council and the reminder to the motoring organisations.

Subsequently, in 1930, the A.A, the R.A.C and the Royal Scottish Automobile Club were allotted their own index marks for this purpose, i.e. QA, QC and QS respectively, although there is no evidence that the latter organisation ever exercised its duties in this respect and the mark QS was later used by the RAC. When the LCC had reached QQ 1000 they re-issued QQ 1001-9999, (by this time long extinct) - apart from the re-use of certain Middlesex marks originally allotted to armoured vehicles this was the only instance of a mass re-use of registrations after 1921.

Further allotments of index marks were made to the three licensing agents through the Q series, up to QT, issued to the AA in 1976. After expiry of this series QX and then QY were used for all three agencies, the letters X and Y being year identifiers to coincide with the X and Y year suffix on normal issues. Additionally an allotment was made in these series to the Royal Air Force Base at Mildenhall, where registration of vehicles belonging to members of the United States Forces in the United Kingdom was undertaken. The format was then reversed with up to four numerals followed by QA, QB etc., the second letter again coinciding with the year prefix currently in use. It should also be mentioned here that the marks QI and QZ were allotted in 1963 to perform the same function in Northern Ireland, but in practice these marks were never brought into use. ZZ, introduced in 1925, performs a similar function in the Republic of Ireland.

[Numbers in the 'Q' series were not issued consecutively, especially by the AA, and there was considerable overlap between the commencement of a new series and the completion of the preceding one. The AA series QM, QP and QT were issued in distinct number blocks, dependent partly upon the make of vehicle and partly upon the shape of the plates, (i.e. whether two squares, two oblong, one oblong and one square, or a single motorcycle plate.)]

No SEX please we're British!

by John Harrison

The British registration system dates back to 1903 and so does its censorship. In 1903 one and two letter codes were allocated to English and Welsh local authorities in order of population size from A to Y and AA to FP. One code was omitted from this sequence, DT on the basis it stood for delirium tremens. As this article will illustrate, what at one time is considered unacceptable subsequently becomes acceptable or vice versa and in 1927 it was decided to allocate DT to the then newly created County Borough, Doncaster, the choice of DT being appropriate as it was, of course, a mnemonic for Doncaster. DD was also omitted as it also stood for a form of alcoholic delirium, but this was allocated to Gloucestershire in 1921.

The final code to be omitted from the original England and Wales allocation was ER, the then royal cipher. This was allocated to Cambridgeshire in 1922. SC, SF, SG, CS, FS & GS were omitted from the Scottish allocation. The likely explanation for this is the possibility of confusing the letters C & G and E and F - at this time most number plates were hand painted, sometimes rather crudely.

Two authorities objected to the codes they were allocated in 1903. The residents of Dorset did not like BF, as this stood for "bloody fool" so this was replaced by FX. The residents of Northampton objected to having DF and they were soon given NH as an alternative code, but in 1927 DF was recommenced after it had been given to Gloucestershire.

As local authorities used up their initial two letter codes, many were allocated further codes. Somewhat surprisingly VD was commenced by Lanarkshire in 1930, though in 1977 Luton LVLO to whom it had then passed stopped issuing three letter codes ending in VD! By the late 1950s only three codes remained unallocated. BF had still not been reused and the other two were OO and WC. Staffordshire and Essex were running short of available registration combinations and BF was allocated to Staffordshire and OO and WC to Essex. BF and WC were only allowed to be used on three letter combinations and the combinations ABF, UBF, AWC and UWC were not allowed. LOO and POO were, however, considered socially acceptable! Despite the ban on BF and WC in the 1950s, some BF's and WC's have now been sold in the government's Classic Auctions!

In the early 1930s local authorities started using three-letter combinations and this obviously produced more scope for rude words. It would take too long to list all banned combinations, but a few obvious examples are FUC, FUK, GOD and SEX. Not all combinations are omitted for reasons of prurience - USN was not used because of possible confusion with US naval registrations and XXX was not used because it was a police radio call sign. DWO was not issued, but nobody has given me an explanation for this. APE is a banned combination but this was actually issued in error by Guildford with T-suffix.

In 1953 reversed registrations were first issued. This only raised two censorship problems. One was the possibility of confusion between the letter "O" and the number "0". To take my own cherished number, 3890 RF, as an example, had 389 ORF also been issued there would have been scope for confusion. Many authorities, Staffordshire who had the RF code included, avoided using letter "triples" commencing with the letter "O". Other authorities, however, used triples commencing with the letter "O", but did not use numbers ending with zero.

The second problem was that trade plates were in the format 123 AB and most local authorities avoided the possibility of confusion by not using the combinations reserved for trade plates. For instance, using RF as an example, this series started at 1000. Other series started at lower numbers, like RE (another Staffordshire code) which started at 500. Recently DVLA has, of course started selling combinations from partially issued series in the Classic Auctions and most such registrations come from these blocks originally reserved for trade plates. The cautious bureaucrats of the 50's and 60's who avoided this duplication have inadvertently managed to provide a bonanza for DVLA as it has meant more low and consequently desirable numbers were available for sale by auction.

The introduction of year letters in 1963 indirectly resulted in another reason for censorship being introduced. Because it became desirable to disguise the age of one's vehicle, cherished numbers became more popular and in the late 1970's.
It became the policy to avoid issuing cherishable numbers as normal registrations, though a few have inevitably slipped through the net over the years, e.g. BEAST, CLA 55Y, NE 55Y, A911 POR and H151 MON (HI SIMON). In 1978/79 combinations ending in xxG IT and xxT IT were withheld, though some examples have been sold in the Classic Auctions, e.g. TAG IT and PUT IT.

When year prefixes commenced in 1983, the numbers 1-20 were withheld for subsequent sale. Also in the "A" year, 55 and 550-9 were not issued for obvious reasons. Around this time most Local Offices stopped issuing "desirable" combinations, e.g. DON, PAM, BMW. Practice has not always been consistent in this respect. For example, Chelmsford withheld SOO when it was due to be issued in the "A" year, but issued it in the "D" and "V" years. Early in the "G" year it was announced that 666 would no longer be issued because of its satanic overtones, though this decision was subsequently reversed in that it can now be purchased under the government's Select scheme.

In 1996 DVLA reviewed the list of banned combinations. Some which were previously banned became available under the Select scheme, ABF, APE, AWC, BBF, BOG, FAG, HOG, LAV, NBG, SOT, and UWC, i.e. one could only be allocated such a registration by deliberately buying it. DWO, GPO which had previously been reserved for Post Office use only and UBF were made generally available.

The new registration system introduced in 2001 has created censorship issues. FO & FU have been completely censored as letter pairs at the beginning of the mark. In addition FK, VD and WC have only been available for purchase under the Select scheme – they are not available as ordinary issues. As with the old system many letter triples have also been banned. Also care has been taken to avoid groupings of letters which become potentially offensive, e.g. AGS, UTS and UTY have not been used in the "51" period and combinations like BU-LLY, DE-ATH and PA-KKY have been banned. Despite this care early in the "02" period Preston Local Office caused offence by issuing PO02 combinations to garages and these were soon withdrawn.

Part Four
The Fun Begins - and never ends

101 fun facts about number plates

Press releases from 2001

People and their plates

Harry Tate,
Music Hall Artist.

1. The world's first national vehicle registration system was introduced in Holland in 1899. Britain followed in 1903. The first plate issued in London, was **A 1**.

2. The earliest known celebrity cherished number plate was **T 8**, owned by Harry Tate (1873-1940), a Music Hall Artist. It is now owned by Johnny Tate of the sugar company Tate & Lyle.

3. Although the number plates **7 ONY** and **CHE 21E** are available, the Prime Minister and his wife are unlikely to buy them, for security reasons.

4. Cherie Blair is reported to have bought a bed for their youngest child Leo, in the shape of a Lamborghini, together with the Downing Street plate **LEO 10**.

5. HM The Queen owns **A 7**, whilst her daughter, Princess Ann used to hold **1 ANN** on her car, but had to take it off for security reasons.

6. HM The Queen Mother had **NLT 2** and her son-in-law HRH Prince Philip has **OXR 1**.

7. **3 GXM** was Princess Margaret's plate and **YR 11** is the Duke of Kent's.

8. **DS 500** is owned by the former Liberal party leader David Steel. I wonder if Jeffrey Archer still owns **ANY 1**.

9. Barry Fry, the manager of 'The Posh' Peterborough FC, bought **POS 11** from dealer Regtransfers.co.uk. He thought David Beckham might like to buy it from

him for his wife Victoria 'Posh Spice', but Becks said she dislikes her nickname. In any case they already own **W77 DVB** and **D7 DVB.**

10. Convicted sex offender, Jonathan King, is reported to have lured boys to his bachelor pad, driving them there in his brown Rolls Royce with the private plate **JK 9000**.

11. Entertainer Max Bygraves, sold his beloved **MB 1** to Regtransfers.co.uk, along with the Rolls Royce it has been on for over 30 years. It has now been sold to a private collector.

12. A Regtransfers.co.uk sales person was sickened to receive an enquiry for the plate **11 SEP**, just days after the terrorist attack in New York.

13. **VIP 1** was originally issued for the Pope's visit to Ireland. Sold by dealer Regtransfers.co.uk in 2001, it is back on the market again.

14. **MG 1** is the most expensive number plate on today's market, priced at a cool £275,000.

15. **MS 1** was first owned by Henry Adolf Salvesen - he acquired it on 28 December 1903. It is on today's market for £250,000.

16. The new style number plates came out on 1st September 2001. Some of the best ones are **DE51 REE**, **LE51 LEY** and **AR51 NAL**.

17. The DVLA have issued many 'naughty' plates: **PU51 SUC, SHA 61N, P9 RNO, EA51 LAY** and even **PEN 15** (bought by Steve Parrish, former British motorcycle champion).

18. The plate **J1 HAD** (Jihad being the Muslim name for a holy war) was banned as soon as the J registrations came out in 1991.

19. Jimmy Tarbuck is the envy of every comedian in the UK with his number plate **COM 1C**.

20. Lennie Bennett, the comedian and television quiz show host, had the last laugh with **GAG 22**.

21. Controversial funny man Bernard Manning owns **BJM 1**, **1 LAF** and **11 LAF**.

22. Mike Reid who played Frank Butcher in Eastenders, owns **JOK 1E**. I wonder if he knows that **JOK 3S** is currently on the market.

23. Sid Owen, who played Frank Butcher's son Ricky, has the plate **360 SYD**.

24. Patsy Palmer, who played Ricky's cheating wife, has **P17 TSY**.

25. Mrs Naseem Hirani from Bristol was delighted when her husband secured the number plate **NA51 EEM** for her. It could make boxer Prince Naseem Hamid wish he'd kept on his toes. He'll have to stick to **NAS 1** for now.

26. **1 KO** and **111 KO** are the knock out number plates of Chris Eubank, supplied by Regtransfers.co.uk

27. Mark Skeggs, a Fireman from Hertfordshire, has the number plate **F14 MES** on his red Ferrari.

28. **POT 73R**, a magical plate for all Harry Potter fans, has come on the market for £15,000.

29. Ventriloquist Keith Harris paid £2,100 for his feathered friend's name plate **ORV 1L**.

30. In the Koran the number 786 has a special religious significance for Muslims who will pay high prices for any plates containing these numbers.

31. In the USA, Vanity Plates, as they call them, are even more popular than in the UK. Nearly any combination is allowed.

32. American fitness club owner Sean Phillips bought **BRA 5H** because he says, he is a 'brash American' now living in England.

33. Kent meat importer Alan Burke's wife Sue refused to get into his car after he bought **ORG 45M**. When it no longer aroused him, he put it up for sale.

34. Leisure company director Linda Downs is happy to drive between her clubs in the Manchester area with the plate **B1 NGO** on her car.

35. Producers of the 20th Bond film, just missed out on the ultimate plate **8 OND**. It was sold in January 2002 to a James Bond fanatic who collects 007 memorabilia.

36. **CUB 1** has featured on a Rolls Royce in a few of the Bond movies. It belonged to the late 007 producer Cubby Brocolli.

37. **1 DLT** is DJ Dave Lee Travis's number. **D1 DDY** is David 'Diddy' Hamilton's.

38. **BS 1** was recently sold to Bill Spence from Orkney, where the plate was first issued. It was owned for many years by Billy Smart (Junior) of circus fame, who gave permission for it to be used in the 70's television series 'The Persuaders'.

39. **FU 2** is owned by Hanna Smart, wife of Billy Smart (Junior). X-rated model Fiona Richmond persuaded Hanna to buy it from Fiona's former boyfriend Paul Raymond (known as the Duke of Soho and owns **PR 11**). Fiona told Hanna she hoped to buy it back from her some day. Hanna still owns it.

40. **S8 RRY** was sold to Robbie Williams for a new Ferrari. 'Sorry' was a message to his fans for spending so much money on a car. He couldn't bring himself to do it in the end and bought a moped instead.

41. In the second episode of the new series of The Vice, two characters had matching Number one plates with their initials - **N1 KFB** and **N1 CFB**, supplied by Regtransfers.co.uk

42. Magician Paul Daniels gets one up on Harry Potter with his **MAG 1C** plate.

43. Snooker legend Joe Davies once owned **CUE 1** and **1 CUE** is currently up for sale.

44. **M19 CUE** is owned by snooker player John Higgins and **CUE 130Y** is owned by Ronnie O'Sullivan.

45. A romantic London Businessman, Stephen Ouvaroff paid £46,500 for **APR 1L** in an auction in 1990. He gave the plate to his wife April.

46. A 1903 De Dion Bouton with the number plate **C 5** completed the London to Brighton run 27 times.

47. Any number plates with the letters SEX have been banned.

48. A Ms. Lenanton of Dorset managed to find a close one though with **S5 EXX**.

49. **B1 BLE** and **J3 SUS** are also forbidden, although it is possible to have **JE51 USX** and **JE51 USC**.

50. Aaron Davies, company director of The One Stop Van Shop in Dunstable, couldn't believe his luck when he found that the number plate **TIL 44** on the car he bought was worth £2,000.

51. The number plate **HER 41D** sold in March 2000 for £2,700. It is now worth nearer £15,000.

52. A 'clever clogs' worked out that if he paid £4,400, he could walk away with the plate **MEN 5A**.

53. Companies love to use cherished number plates to advertise their name, such as the whiskey company that owns **VAT 69**.

54. The Pimlico Plumbers in London are collecting number plates for their company vans. So far they have bought **DRA 1N**, **LAV 1** and **BOG 1**.

55. **1 KEG** and **A1 KEG** were bought by Alan and David Morrow of Morrow Brothers Ltd, the largest seller of stainless steel beer kegs in the UK.

56. A company in Sussex, D. Sankey Pest Control Services own **M1 CES**, **M1 TES** and **L1 CES**, amongst others, as an investment.

57. Patrick Clacy's upmarket bed business 'And so to bed' in the centre of Oxford bought **CO51 BED** for the company van.

58. Although **F15 ONS** has never been released, **BUX 70N** has - a perfect number for the British mineral water company.

59. **GEN 11** was used on the car Chitty Chitty Bang Bang in the film of the same name.

60. **GEN 22** was bought by a man from Lancashire, for the replica he is building of the Chitty Chitty Bang Bang car.

61. **FAB 1**, another famous plate was used on Lady Penelope's pink Rolls Royce in Thunderbirds.

62. **ST 1** was used in the series The Saint, on a Volvo P1800 sports car.

63. Phillip Haslam from Derbyshie was astonished to find the plate **ALW 1** in a Regtransfers advert, originally belonging to his 1933 Aston Martin le Mans, both of which were first owned by Sir Malcolm Campbell.

64. **B1 LKO** was bought at auction by a fan of the TV series.

65. British actor and director, Richard Attenborough, knighted in 1976 and made a Lord in 1994, owns **RA 1**.

66. Richard Pearson from Lincolnshire is going where no man has gone before at Warp 8 speed in his Honda Accord with the plate **W4 RPB**.

67. **5 POK** was not bought by Star Trek fans, but by Mr and Mrs Borkett, from Bedfordshire, for their alien looking dog called Spok.

68. Michael Christie thought that the plate **M4 TCH** would suit his 10 year old football mad son Myles. Myles said "It's a really cool plate because it is about football - and that's my life."

69. Soccer star Robbie Fowler missed out on the plate **FOW 13R** last year, and he'll have to hurry to secure **ROB 131E** because Robbie Williams is already interested.

70. **7 SM** is owned by Stirling Moss. His lucky number is 7, which he had on his racing cars whenever he could. On Easter Monday 1962, his yellow Lotus went careering out of control at 140mph, on the Goodwood race circuit. **777 M** was later specially issued to him.

71. The late Rob Walker, who witnessed the fatal car crash of his friend Mike Hawthorne, Britain's first Formula One World Champion, owned **ROB 2**, **R 8** and **E 53**.

72. Rob had also secured **ND 1** for his Father-in-law, Mr. N. Duncan. He had to return it when it was found that it had already been issued to Nora Docker of the wealthy banking family.

73. The Registration Numbers Club (RNC) was founded in 1977 following two civil service unions imposing a ban on number plate transfers. After intense lobbying by dealers and cherished number plate owners, the dispute was resolved and new rules were introduced. The changes included the government introducing legislation to permit cherished transfers.

74. The ban on transferring plates from motorbikes and mopeds to cars was lifted in October 2001.

75. A father from Cornwall bought a pair of plates, **WET 1** and **1 WET** as a sound investment for his children, with money left by their grandparents.

76. Kriss Akabusi, Gold Medallist in the 1990 European Championships when he beat David Hemery's 22-year-old British Record, purchased a 'Mister' plate with his initials, **M12 KDA**.

77. Ex-Aston Villa Manager, John Gregory paid £44,000 for **V1 LLA** in 2000.

78. Doug Ellis, Chairman of Aston Villa F.C. owns **AV 1**.

79. **AFC 1** is owned by Arsenal Football Club and one of their biggest fans recently bought **AR51 NAL**.

80. **1 TEL** is the number plate of former England football coach, Terry Venables. **TEL 1** was brought recently by a man from Essex.

81. Footballer Dwight Yorke was hoping that Hastings Borough Council would sell him **DY 1**, but they have said it is no longer for sale. He will have to settle for **Y10 RKE** or **Y9 RKE**.

82. Man United footballer Andy Cole owns **C6 LES** and **C9 LEY** but missed out on **C8 LEY**, which was bought by a Mr. Ian Cole from South Humberside.

83. Roy Keane of Man United also owns a couple of plates: **111 RK** and **J60 ROY**. Perhaps **K3 ANE** or **1 UTD** were a bit too pricey for him.

84. **S4 LEM** sold at auction in 2002 for $10,800 after 'fierce and rapid bidding. Salem has Biblical and Welsh connections and in English means 'Peace'. **80 SS** (Boss) sold just after for £31,000.

85. Top Jockey Leofranco (Franki) Dettori's number is **X777 LEO**.

86. Iwan Thomas, Olympic 400m Gold Medallist owns **R400 RUN**. His team mates Katharine Merry and Jamie Baulch recently followed suit with **M400 RUN** and **J400 RUN**.

87. Former champion jockey Willie H. Carson will no longer have problems recognising his Isuzu Trooper in a field of 4x4's, now that he has added his own unique personal number plate, **N1 WHC** to the vehicle.

88. On 14 December 1989, **1 A** fetched £160,000 at auction.

89. A suitable plate for material girl Madonna is **M4 DGE** - shame the Pop Queen hates her nickname.

90. Ivan Scott from Burnley in Lancashire owns the ultimate England Cricket ground plate, **OVA 1**.

91. **E6 YPT** was bought at auction for £5,000, but **J4 PAN** is still on the market at £15,000.

92. Former Kent and England fast bowler Dean Headley had to retire at the young age of 33 due to a back injury. He purchased **M12 DML** to go with his new company Deano Management Ltd.

93. Perhaps his friend, England Cricket Captain, Nasser Hussain will be bowled over by **NA51 SER** or **HUS 541N**.

94. Paul Sissons from Derby bought **D3 RBY** because he is very proud to come from Derby and is mad about the football club.

95. John Savage from Peterborough got his **UND 1S** in a twist when he saw this plate. The avid memorabilia collector proudly displays it on his Ford Thunderbird.

96. In 1990, Haggis maker David A. Hall Ltd from Dumfries in Edinburgh, paid £18,000 for **HAG 1S**.

97. Jon Culverhouse from Luton says that his plate **5 NOV** is excellent for promoting his business, Fantastic Fireworks.

98. Mr. and Mrs. Beresford from Cheshire promised their daughter Zoe that if she never took up smoking they would buy her a car for her 17th birthday. They bought her a new style VW Beetle with the plate **DO51 ZOE**.

99. Devoted parents Stuart and Teresa Taylor from Gloucester bought their son Otis a number plate with his initials, **920 FRT**, for his 21st birthday. Except Otis is only three! They said it is a good long-term investment.

100. Mr. Neufville from Hertfordshire took 20 years to find his ideal 'Mister' number plate with his initials, **M12 SPN**.

101. The aristocratic **10 RD**, **14 DY** and **BUT 13R** plates prove that three is not always a crowd.

Press Releases

Press Releases issued by Regtransfers during 2001

A utopig.co.uk, the UK's market leaders when it comes to buying or selling your vehicle Free online, have added the finishing touch to its company branded Smart Car, with its own personalised registration number "11 OG" (HOG).

When Autopig.co.uk was planning its launch in February, it turned to Registration Transfers to give its promotional Smart Car a mark that would add to its quirky pig theme. The unique Autopig logo of a smiling pig wearing sun glasses, positioned looking out of the middle of a tyre, has a slot in its head to signify the 'saving you money' concept behind the unique Autopig service.

Autopig's Managing Director, John Doherty, was delighted with the choice: "I drive the car to and from the office every day, and it's great to see the positive reaction to the new plate. It is the perfect marketing tool for getting our company noticed."

John told Tony Brown, the proprietor of Registration Transfers that he was looking for a number plate with a distinctive pig theme. He was pleased to find that he had several to choose from: X1 HOG; HOG 999; V1 HOG and P1 GAG (PIG AG). A number of plates with a swine theme have been sold by Registration Transfers in recent years: P16 GYS (PIGGYS); P16 HAM (PIG HAM); P16 SHT (PIG SHIT) and P16 ART (PIG ART).

But 11 OG just stood out above the rest for Autopig. They certainly know how to "HOG" the limelight!

9 June 2001

Recently retired, Kent and England fast bowler Dean Headley is already making a comeback - in a new business venture. After being forced to bow out of cricket on medical grounds just a few weeks ago, Dean has already set up his own Design and Print Company, called 'IDP'. Dean brings the new business under the umbrella of his existing company 'DML' (Deano Management Ltd), which is now a representative of IDP (also of Walker Logistics).

Based at private premises in Canterbury, Dean's role as Director of DML is to promote the newly formed IDP and generate business. With this task in mind he decided to search for a personalised number plate on the Registration Transfers website, www.regtransfers.co.uk

Although always interested in having a personalised number plate, Dean says it "goes against his personality" to have a mark spelling his name. He wanted something much more subtle; a plate to advertise his parent company so that only people close to him or people who know of DML would recognise it.

Dean was particularly taken with the 'M12' (Mr) numbers, and was delighted when he found 'M12 DML' (Mr. DML). He said, "I think Mr DML is a good plate to have. I am very pleased with it. It will help me to get the company name known".

The Marketing Manager at Registration Transfers, Len Stout, commented: "The 'MR' number plates are very popular with customers who are looking for something a bit different, in particular Managing Directors' who are keen to personalise their vehicles. They tend to add either the company's initials or their own initials after 'MR'."

Dean has also bought G8 DML (GB DML) to complement his mister plate. Staff at Registration Transfers in Dunstable were keen to find him the perfect match. Dean said it was "fantastic" when informed that a 'Great Britain' number was found with 'DML'. But will he make it a hat trick, they wonder!

1 June 2001

Posh plumbers pu|

Pimlico Plumbers, twice voted the UK's top domestic heating and plumbing engineers as National Domestic Installers of the Year, has combined excellent technical skills and a fast, efficient service to establish itself as the benchmark for how a business should be run.

Pimlico's most recent achievement for their high profile publicity, was winning the H & V "2001 Marketing Incentive of the Year", to which of course their personalised registrations contributed.

Part of the company's success is its attention to detail both in the appearance of its staff and the livery of its fleet of 56 Volkswagen vans, but two vehicles have been made even more distinctive with the addition of the plumber's ultimate personalised registrations, BOG 1 and LAV 1.

Pimlico Plumbers had already purchased DRA 1N from Registration Transfers, Britain's largest supplier of special registration numbers, and now with the acquisition of BOG 1 and LAV 1, two more of their vehicles have become a little more distinctive and memorable - it also has the additional element of fun.

Pimlico Plumbers Managing Director Charlie Mullins was "delighted" to find the plates and how Registration Transfers took care of all the details: "Registration Transfers handled the sale and transfer of our registrations, once again with superb efficiency, from the initial search to the completion of all relevant documentation. These plates have added a touch of recognition and fun to our vans and our customers are always commenting on them. That means they never forget who we are."

Pimlico Plumbers has carved a niche for itself by concentrating its efforts in an area of just 3 square miles of Central London, but one that contains some of the most expensive properties and historic buildings in the capital. This means that presenting the right image to customers, who expect to receive the very best service and the highest of standards, is essential. Distinctive number plates provide the finishing touch.

114

Pimlico Plumbers joins Registration Transfers' ever-growing list of businesses that use cherished registration plates to make their vehicles more distinctive. The company's web site at www.regtransfers.co.uk has 19 specialist searches, one of which is SuperSearch™. This search facility interrogates their huge database of millions to find a fully personalised choice of registrations.

For the client's peace of mind, Registration Transfers is a member of the C.N.D.A (Cherished Number Dealers Association) and the R.M.I. (Retail Motor Industry Federation) and as such abide by their strict codes of conduct.

2 June 2001

Registration Transfers provide 'M4 TCH' mark for footballing son

For Michael Christie, finding a personal number plate that says 'M4TCH' (Match) was the ultimate gift for his 10 year old son, Myles, from Bedfordshire. Michael originally rang local Cherished Number Plate dealer, Registration Transfers, looking for a plate that said "Myles", but after 'M4TCH' was suggested to him, Michael came away with a far more eye-catching mark that even the highest paid Premier League Footballers can only dream of.

Michael, an avid Arsenal supporter, said it was appropriate, "because I take my son to and from loads of football matches, and it looks to people like I am a footballer!" When asked if he would sell the plate to a Premier League player, he said, "I would certainly consider it!" Myles plays for local team St. Martins and said, "it is a cool plate because it is about footy - and that's my life."

13 June 2001

A number plate for a dog? - it's completely illogical Captain!

For the Borkett family from Bedfordshire, the number plate '5 POK' (Spock) was very much a logical choice for their much-loved Doberman. The lanky-legged canine was a rescue dog that they named 'Spok' because they thought he looked very "alienesque" with his extra long legs and very pointy ears (when flipped back!)

Surprisingly perhaps, there are no Star Trek fans in this family: "We wanted the plate just for the dog, we are not Trekkies", insisted Mr and Mrs Borkett, "The plate brings smiles to people's faces. One man even said, 'Does Spock know you have his car?' "

Star Trek devotees everywhere, and even Mr. Spock himself would think that buying a number plate for a pet dog certainly was illogical, yet at Registration Transfers, where the Borketts bought their alien mark, sales of personalised plates to dog lovers is not uncommon. For instance, 'R8 ROT', was bought by Mr. Howell from
Wiltshire for his two Rottweilers: "We are now the envy of the Rott fraternity", he said. Likewise, 'A800 PUG', was bought by Mr. Jackman from Anglesey for his two pet Pugs and 'A9 DOG' was bought by Mrs Purcell from Surrey "because I love dogs and I have two cross-terriers."

20 June 2001

A personalised number plate is a g

Personalised number plates have historically increased their value over the years, but now it seems that people are choosing to buy them instead of investing their hard earned cash in ISA's, TESSA's and the new Baby Bond ®.

Devoted parents Stuart and Teresa Taylor from Gloucester recently bought their son Otis an unusual 21st birthday present – a personalised number plate. But even more unusual is that they have bought it 18 years early – little Otis is only three!

"We thought it would be a good long-term investment and were sure he would be pleased with it when the time comes, although he does refer to it as his already."

The last four characters of the number plate, 920 FRT, spell Otis's full name: Otis Fenton Robert Taylor. Though the Taylors admit: "we were originally looking for a plate for either of us, or one that referred to our newly opened Trout Lake, but when this one came up we thought it was perfect."

Regtransfers.co.uk have a special search engine built into the website, which allowed the Taylors to look through all their options quickly and efficiently. By typing personal details such as name and birth date into SuperSearch ™, all the options matching their unique information combinations came up straight away.

Likewise, a couple from Hampshire have bought the number plate V8 MJP for their four-month-old son, again purely as an investment for their child's future.

But some people buy and sell number plates almost as if they were stocks and shares! Ivan Scott from Burnley, Lancashire, buys number plates primarily for enjoyment but says, "they are also most definitely an investment". For instance, he purchased 11 YS for his daughter Yasmin's 11th birthday and 1 VY which was his nickname, for himself. He later sold 1 VY for a tidy profit. His latest purchase is 3 VN, which he says "makes his new BMW convertible look more prestigious."

Motoring commentator Quentin Willson has also noticed this growing trend, as he described in his article 'Crazy Prices' in The Mirror back in May while visiting a number plate auction: "What struck me as most interesting is the fact that ordinary people are buying these plates as investments." He went on to describe how an electrician who was sitting next to him, was buying up cheap plates on his day off to sell on to his friends for twice the price!

Even private companies are joining the rush to buy up desirable number plates with the belief that they will be worth more in the future. A pest control company in Uckfield, Sussex, D. Sankey Pest Control Services, and the 'posh' Pimlico Plumbers in London, have gone one stage further – buying a whole set of number plates to suit their businesses. Sankey's vans are riddled with infestation: M1 CES, L1 CES, M1 TES, ANT 7T, A3 FLY and W4 SPS amongst others, commanding a current value of £55,000. David Sankey said "I would like it if eventually someone bought the whole lot from me."

15 August 2001

C athy 'The Bitch' Brown, women's flyweight boxing champion is determined to knock 'em dead - with her new personalised number plate 'B17 CHX' ('Bitch X'). Cathy, who works out at the Kronk gym in Kentish Town, London, will be fighting Ionela Zgulea of Romania on a big boxing night at the Wembley Conference Centre on Saturday 16th June 2001. She will be joining fellow female boxer, Jane 'The Fleetwood Assassin' Couch and heading the bill is the legendary "ButterBean" from the U.S., fighting in Europe for the first time.

The plate fits in perfectly with Cathy's boxing nickname: 'The Bitch'. "Everyone around here knows me - and now when they see my plate, they know it is me driving past - it is excellent for self-promotion".

Cathy only started boxing two years ago, after enjoying a successful eight-year career in kick boxing. In the short time Cathy has been involved in classic boxing, she has already reached the world number one ranking in female flyweight boxing as well as becoming WBF European Flyweight Champion.

When asked how she deals with all the controversy surrounding women 'fighting', she said: "I just ignore all of that and get on with it." She considers herself a pioneer of women's boxing, "There are only five of us in the country - it's got to start somewhere."

Cathy was pleased when she found her favourite mark on the Registration Transfers website (www.regtransfers.co.uk) and said she would recommend its search facilities to anyone, "It was an excellent way of finding the plate that I was looking for", said Cathy, "I think it's a knock out site!"

4 June 2001

Top marks for the ne\

The UK's largest Cherished Number Plate dealer, Registration Transfers, has launched it's summer collection of new style personal number plates, on their website: www.regtransfers.co.uk

The new style is being introduced by the DVLA from 1 September 2001, following its purge during the month of May of the new '51' series. RegTransfers, scrambled to secure the best of the new style registrations. Joseph Randlesome, Business Development Manager at RegTransfers said he was "very pleased that we can now offer customers the best of the new plates, for example: 'AR51 NEL' (Arsenal); 'DE51 REE' (Desiree) 'UR51 ULA' (Ursula) and 'BO51 EYS' (Bosley's)"

The new Vehicle Number Plate system comprises seven characters in the following order: two letters, two numbers, a space, and then three letters. The first two letters are the local office identifier. For instance BD would denote Birmingham and OA would denote Oxford etc.

The two numbers in the middle are the age identifiers. For the six-month period between September 2001 and February 2002, this number will be 51. This could become a little confusing in March 2002, when the number combination will change to 02. It will change again in September 2002 to 52 and so on. It appears that the DVLA have decided to hold back the 01 numbers for a rainy day.

The original idea back in March 2000, was to have the age identifier 01, for cars bought in September 2001. "It certainly rules out some potentially excellent plates!" said Mr. Randlesome, who was surprised at the recent decision not to use the 01 numbers. The last three letters are random, meaning that the whole plate could look like this: BD51 SMR.

The idea behind the changes is to make it easier for the public to memorise the plates, which in turn will help police identify offenders. A standard style of lettering will also be used for the same reason so that plates can be read by speed cameras. The regulations will end the use of italic, 3D, multiple strokes and other lettering on number plates.

18 June 2001

F U2 is one of the most notorious cherished number plates on the market today. Steeped in celebrity history, the plate makes the kind of statement that would make your granny's hair curl!

Whoever buys it from the current owners, Billy and Hanna Smart (of Big Top Circus fame) they will have to be daring enough to carry it off, because, as Hanna Smart maintains, "it attracts all kinds of attention." Indeed, Hanna recalls probably the most awkward moment in FU2's colourful history, when the Queen, accompanied by two body guards rode past Hanna as she stood in Windsor Great Park with her Range Rover which was sporting the cheeky plate. As Hanna felt the flush of embarrassment, she says she couldn't tell whether Her Highness was amused or not!

Despite this, Hanna Smart recalls many gloriously happy times driving around with the FU2 plate. She says: "It's a conversation piece. Most of the time I forgot it was there until someone would call out to me. Usually they'd call: 'Fiona, Fiona'. I think they thought I was Fiona Richmond!" The plate was previously owned by Soho nightclub owner Paul Raymond, who's one time girlfriend, Fiona Richmond, a blonde actress, had the plate on her primrose yellow E-type Jag. When the couple parted, Fiona persuaded Billy to buy it for Hanna with a view to eventually buying it back.

In the early days, Hanna says that the police seemed particularly taken by the saucy plate, even pulling her over and following her home just so they could ask her about it. Now she has had the plate for 25 years, won't she miss it? – "Its time to let someone else have some fun with it now!" Hanna says with a knowing smile, "the number plate is rude in a way, but I don't think of it as rude – I think of it as fun."

Billy and Hanna's children, Billy-Jay and Baccara, are the ones that tend to drive round with the plate these days – it is currently on the family Merc. Though Billy-Jay warns, "it's not the best plate when you want to go out and not be seen. One time a news camera crew spotted it, so it was shown on the local news, and I was somewhere where I wasn't supposed to be!"

The Smarts are also selling another part of their family history – their BS1 plate. It was purchased in the 1960's by the late Billy Smart (senior). Billy-Jay said: "my father gave permission for BS1 to be used in the early 1970's television series, The Persuaders. It was the perfect plate for the Aston Martin which was driven by Roger Moore's character - the English gent, Brett

Sinclair." It has been on Billy's striking purple Rolls Royce Corniche convertible since the early 70's. Billy remembers the trouble he had persuading Rolls Royce to spray a car such an outlandish colour, "I told them if they wanted my business, then they would have to sell me a car the colour I wanted."

The Smarts' decided to turn to Registration Transfers for their expert help in selling BS1 and FU2. Marketing Manager, Len Stout said: "We are very pleased to work for the Smarts' as sole agents. As the UK's largest number plate dealer, and with the kind of marketing we do here at RegTransfers, we are confident that we can find buyers for both plates."

23 June 2001

T he UK's largest Cherished Number Plate dealer, Registration Transfers, has launched it's latest advertising drive, this time on television and radio.

"This is a new area of advertising for us," said Len Stout, Marketing Manager at RegTransfers, "we already advertise extensively in the national newspapers, car magazines and on the web, but we thought that we would try out a different medium. We like to think of different ways of staying the UK's largest dealer."

The television advert is currently running on Granada TV and goes out during 'Men and Motors', three days a week. Brocket Hall in Hertfordshire provided an excellent backdrop for the yellow Alpha Spider which was used in the filming.

The ad begins with a standard number plate shown on the car, but as the car sweeps round the drive in front of Brocket Hall, it is suddenly sporting the much more appropriate CLA 5S number plate. Without any fuss, it shows the kind of transformation that can be made to a car with a quality personalised number plate. "We pride ourselves on selling the best quality number plates on the market today", Len maintains.

The radio advertising is being run on Chiltern radio (96.9). The domain name Numberplates.com, which is owned by RegTransfers, was used instead of regtransfers.co.uk because it is easier to understand over the air waves. The quirky 20 second commercial, which goes out six times a day, explains to listeners that there is a number plate for everyone from as little as £300.

"I like the idea of TV and radio advertising because of the involuntary listening time that it provides - people don't switch off during the adverts, and even if they are not consciously watching or listening, they are still absorbing the information.

We want to target those people who may never have thought about or dreamed of owning a number plate before. Our excellent sales staff can help them find a suitable mark - we firmly believe that there is something for everyone."

29 June 2002

For leading cherished number plate dealer, Regtransfers.co.uk, having the best footballing marks available is just another part of its excellent service. Their website www.regtransfers.co.uk is definitely the first port of call.

Click on 'Football' to view the dedicated football page, and it will show a drop-down menu of all the football clubs around. Once you have selected the football club of your choice, click on the button 'click here to search'. The database pulls up every conceivable number plate to do with that club. For instance if Manchester United football club is selected, the results range from A1 RED, G7 GGS, K3 ANE to Y9 RKE and even 1 UTD - a wide selection for fans and players alike!

One fan recently added his new D3 RBY plate to his Jaguar XKR Convertible. He bought the number plate because it is his birthplace, but also because: "I'm proud of the city and I'm mad about Derby County FC."

Popularity for number plates with a football theme is definitely growing. Other Football number plates currently available are: AR51 NEL, AR51 NHL, AR51 NAL, LE51 AUX, Y10 RKE, WE51 HAM, S8 URS, B8 URY and S6 ORED. Come on you fans!

27 July 2001

29 June 2001

The great name search from Regtransfers.co.uk

A n excellent new search facility for Christian names and Surnames has been launched by the number one cherished number plate dealer, Regtransfers.co.uk.

Simply click on the title 'Is Your Name Available?' from the comprehensive list on the Regtransfers homepage www.regtransfers.co.uk and it will take you to a simple search facility where you can type in either your first name or your last name.
When you click on the 'Find your ideal plate!' button, your options will appear instantly. Examples of names that are available through the Regtransfers.co.uk site are: LE 3 (Lee); J4 MES (James); A1 ANS (Alan's); SON 1A (Sonia); BES 3 (Bess); B3 TSY (Betsy); 8 OYD (Boyd); MAR 1A (Maria); N1 ALL (Niall) and D6 YLE (Doyle).

The new service complement's the long-standing 'Plates Like Names' page, which allows you to select the first letter of your name, bringing up a long list of possibilities. Business Development Manager at Regtransfers.co.uk, Joseph Randlesome

said: "Whilst the 'Plates Like Names' page is excellent because it's so comprehensive, we felt that there was a need for our customers to be able to have a more specific search for their individual names. After all, one of the most popular personalised number plate types is the name plate. 'Is Your Name Available' is proving to be a very popular addition to the website."

25 July 2001

New era spells new PO51BILITIES for personalised number plates

A t leading personalised number plate dealer, Regtransfers.co.uk in Dunstable, the atmosphere is buzzing with excitement and anticipation at the official beginning of the new era for personal registrations on 1 September 2001.

It is the first major change in the system since February 1963 when the "suffix" registrations were first used. In August 1983, the "prefix" system replaced it until the last letter 'Y' (which came out in march), completed this combination, and the new system was conceived.

The business of number plates started with The Motor Car Act of 1903 after complaints from road users about the dismal state of the country's roads. The introduction of taxing vehicles came in to fund the road improvements. The first vehicle registration fee was set at 20 shillings with a driver's licence fee of 5 shillings.

It was about the same time that it was becoming apparent that because so many cars were now on the road, efforts needed to be made to register and identify vehicles. Henry Ford's now infamous quote: "You can have any colour as long as it's black", only added to the confusion. Whether intentionally or not, you could park your "dirty" Ford behind a much cleaner one, go about your business and quite innocently take the car in front, believing it to be yours.

Now is the best time to find a bargain. You can have a number plate with your full name or initials at a very reasonable price. Regtransfers have already sold EU51 ACE to a Mr. Eustace, CO51 BED to a bed company, NA51 EEM to Mrs Naseem Hirani from Bristol, JA51 PAL to a man in Middlesex, MR51 OCK to a Mrs. Lock, MR51 AKE to a Mrs Lake, AN51 ELL to a Mrs. Ansell and LE51 LEY to a man in Cheshire. Their highest priced new style plate is DE51 REE at a cool £9,995. Regtransfers expect the market to increase further after tomorrow. It is a very exciting time for this industry.

1 September 2001

Mr. Neufville from Letchworth in Hertfordshire has been looking for a number plate with his initials, S.P.N. for over twenty years! Searching through lists of number plates in the Sunday newspapers had become part of his weekly routine until he decided to telephone the UK's premier number plate dealer, Regtransfers.co.uk, to see if they could help him.

One of the top sales women at Regtransfers.co.uk, Simone Davies, took Mr. Neufville's call. "After explaining to me that he was looking for a number plate that included his initials SPN, I asked Mr. Neufville what his budget was. I checked through our computerised network system, and recommended the M12 and M15 style plates, which are a very popular, fun and an inexpensive way of owning a personalised number plate."

Mr. Seaford Patrick Neufville didn't want a plate with PAT or PN, which perhaps would have been the most obvious choices. Instead, he says: "The 'Mister' plate M12 SPN was an excellent idea, much more subtle, and one that I had not considered before. Top marks to Regtransfers for such helpful sales staff!"

After a search that has been as enduring as his marriage, Mr. Neufville bought the number plate as a 25th wedding anniversary present - to himself! It now sits proudly on his immaculate black Honda Prelude. We certainly think he deserves it and he definitely thinks it was worth the wait!

20 August 2001

Passionate fireman in F14 MES over hot number plate!

S elf-confessed car fanatic, Mark Skeggs, from Hertfordshire has found the perfect number plate to emblazon on his red Ferrari 308GT4 - F14 MES! This passion for fast cars was started by his late Father, James.

Mark says he has always liked to make up words and names from car registration plates and, so it is no surprise that he decided to invested in F14 MES. "I found this excellent plate on the Regtransfers.co.uk website. It was rather appropriate for me because I am a Fireman and I also own a racing car which does actually make flames."

Having spent around 2,000 hours working on just one car, Mark says "This is when being a Fireman comes in handy as it gives me the time off I need to ensure the cars are in top condition."

Mark has been through ARDS training for duties at Ferrari Owners Club days, which means that he is qualified to teach on track, giving his M. S. Racing (Mark Skeggs Racing) Corporate and Business clients the assurance that they are getting a certified standard of driving and instruction. "The number plate completes the executive look of the car, helping to make it a desirable and ultimate driving experience for all of my clients."

F14 MES joins an ever-growing list of plates that match the owner's profession. Top salesman at Regtransfers.co.uk, Barry Tuck, says "I have sold DRA 1N to the Pimlico Plumbers in London, F1 ASH, to an electrician in Surrey, and now F14 MES to a fireman! We have also sold D1 HOT to a Mr. Souness, who also owns a 'hot' Ferrari!"

18 December 2001

Parents buy DO51 ZOE a new car for not taking up smoking

D evoted parents, Mr. and Mrs. Beresford from Cheshire told their daughter Zoë from a very young age that if she made sure that she never smoked cigarettes, they would buy her a brand new car when she reached 17 years old.

Zoë is now 17 and is looking forward to receiving her brand new VW Beetle on January 1st. To add the finishing touch, Mr. Beresford decided to buy Zoë a personalised number plate to go with it. He looked on the Regtransfers website, www.regtransfers.co.uk, where they have a special section called 'New Style Regs' and by using the drop down menu's, found a huge selection of new style number plates.

"She had a choice," Mr. Beresford explained, "between DO51 ZOE (Dozy Zoë); ME51 ZOE (Messy Zoë); PO51 ZOE (Posy Zoë) and LA51 ZOE (Lazy Zoë). She is a bit of a dozy Zoë, so it had to be that one! It wasn't easy to get a number plate with Zoë on before, but now with the new style number plates there are several to choose from. I just had to get her one before they all went! She is thrilled with the plate and can't wait to see it on her new car. It is well deserved."

Mr. Beresford said that although he hadn't bought the number plate as an investment, but he was hoping that it would hold its value.

Marketing Manager, Len Stout said, "The new style registration plates spell some excellent names, such as DE51 REE, RO51 MAY, NA51 EEM, JA51 PER and AU51 TEN. We have many 'SU51' plates for sale, which are proving to be very popular amongst the girl's names, for instance SU51 SSS, SU51 TTT and SU51 COX. People are choosing the combinations they want instead of being restricted by the first two letters they would be given in their part of the country. And they are shrewdly buying before the big number plate change on September 1st to avoid disappointment."

22 August 2001

16 Years with NA51 EEM

The new style number plates are proving to be more popular than anyone first imagined. And there are bargains to be had if you shop early. With a bit of foresight, it is possible to pick up a number plate that could quickly be worth more money almost instantly.

But there could be big disappointments for some, for instance the boxer Prince Naseem Hamed would have to pay a lot of money to persuade Mrs. Naseem Hirani from Bristol to part with her new treasure, NA51 EEM!

On 29th September, it was Mr. and Mrs. Hirani's 16th wedding anniversary. To celebrate in a big way, Mr. Hirani decided to buy his wife a new style number plate with her name on it. "I am very lucky to get the number plate. My husband happened to be browsing through the newspapers one day, and saw this listed in the Regtransfers.co.uk advert. My husband said he had to buy it for me. I was so excited! We should be thanking Regtransfers really!" said Mrs Hirani.

The number plate will be a cherished reminder of their happy years together. It will be going on a new Vauxhall Corsa at the end of September. Top sales woman at Regtransfers.co.uk, Justine Burman, dealt with Naseem Hirani. "I received excellent service from Justine, and your payment arrangements have been very helpful to us."

30 August 2001

Don't get your UND 1S in a twist

John Savage from Wittering in Peterborough, who has an eye for the 'unusual and out of the ordinary', has added the personalised number plate UND 1S to his ever growing collection.

"I do not work in the lingerie world, but I do collect 50's and early 60's memorabilia - anything from cars, clothes, records, jukeboxes, the list goes on and on. I admit that I have sold a few 50's net underskirts to women who require period items of clothing. It causes some amusing comments!" John owns several number plates, including 7 FNP, 4242 PP, TRL 331, as well as UND 1S. He has an impressive car collection to match: 55 Ford Consul, a Ford Thunderbird, Chevy Camero and a Pontiac Transam. "Over the years the house and garages have become more and more like a museum. It does have its benefits though, I am sometimes asked to put my collection on display in public libraries, museums, schools and car shows."

"I started the collection when I was still at school and at that time it wasn't even collectable. I was one of the original 'Teddy Boy's' and I have even kept my suit, which still fits me today! I think that times were easier in those days, no stress like we all have today. I sometimes attend the original 50's Rock 'n' Roll dances at the Thunderbird Club in Wellingborough. If you don't turn up in 50's clothes, you stand out like a sore thumb - it's like stepping back into my old school days. I seem to just go to work to earn money to feed my obsession of that era!"

"I phoned Regtransfers just to get my registrations valued. I spoke to Justine Burman - who was very helpful. She asked me if I collected number plates, and when I said I did, she told me about UND 1S and I thought, how unusual, and decided to buy it and sell 7 FNP. I am convinced that I must be an attention seeker, what with the cars and registrations. I must admit they do attract lots of comments!"

8 October 2001

Football number plate trend continues at RegTransfers.co.uk

Luton (and Republic of Ireland under 21 International) footballer striker, Liam George, is the latest to join the growing number of soccer stars buying up personalised number plates from RegTransfers.co.uk

"I wanted to have my name on a plate, and first looked on the website www.regtransfers.co.uk for L1 AMG, (Liam G), but found L14 MBG instead, which is brilliant because it includes all my initials, plus it only cost £395." Liam (Brendon) George is pleased that he is joining the country's biggest football personalities in this growing number plate trend. "I think I will have to start this craze with the rest of the Luton team now!"

Marketing Manager, Len Stout said, "It is also the football fans that are buying number plates to suit their team, such as Paul Sisson from Derby who purchased D3 RBY and Suzanne and Darren Spalding who purchased EN51 GER and GB51 GER from us following the historic England win against Germany recently. The interest is certainly growing."

As a child, Liam's football hero was Chris Waddle who played for Tottenham Hotspur, "I always aspired to be as good as him when I was growing up". Waddle also purchased the plate WAD 8 from Regtransfers.

Liam is also lucky enough to have 'footballing' names, like the legendary Ireland players before him: Liam Brady and George Best. "I was actually named after Liam Brady, so my ambition is to move up to the senior Republic of Ireland team and live up to my namesake."

So it seems that Liam was destined for football and perhaps also destined to have a private number plate! Liam has put the new mark on his purple Peugeot 306 convertible and says he is looking forward to the teams' reaction when he turns up for training with his new plate, "I'm sure they'll all want one!"

Having just sold FOW 13R (Fowler) at Regtransfers.co.uk, could another footballing star have already snapped up his name on a plate?

20 September 2001

Regtransfers.co.uk supplies 'The Vice' with No.1 plates

The popular and critically acclaimed drama The Vice, set in the vice unit of the Metropolitan Police, is back for a new series in January.

Created by executive producer Rob Pursey and writer Barry Simner for Carlton Television, the hard-hitting programme, now in its fourth series, is eagerly awaited by viewers.

For the villainous husband and wife characters in the second episode, Stephen Smallwood, Producer, decided their cars, a Bentley and a Lexus 4x4, needed to have matching personalised number plates. He approached top number plate dealer, RegTransfers.co.uk, to see if they could help out.

Marketing Manager Len Stout said "We are very pleased to have been asked to supply number plates for The Vice. We found a matching 'Number One' pair (N1) followed by each of the characters initials - N1 KFB and N1 CFB, both of which RegTransfers.co.uk own. The television appearance will certainly give the plate's added interest and a touch of notoriety, and when someone comes to buy them - and it will give them a story to tell their friends! We will of course be explaining to any potential purchaser that the plates are booked to appear in The Vice for the second episode. N1 number plates are one of the most popular types of personalised number plates that we sell. "

20 December 2001

Tears of joy when number plate is found

An eye-catching number plate, 2 CRY brought tears of joy to Nigel Lowe, A & R boss at London based 'Cry Records' when he set eyes on it. He just couldn't believe his eyes.

Nigel recently purchased the number plate from Regtransfers.co.uk, and he says, "It's a great plate to be seen with and fantastic for the company image. I saw it advertised as I surfed the internet and thought it would be the perfect 'on the move' promotion for Cry Records."

The number plate is currently assigned to Nigel's smart Porsche Boxster, and he welcomes the attention it draws. Cry Records is a young company based in Covent Garden. The company searches for new talent to sign and contract out to the major labels. "In the image-obsessed world of pop, standing out from a crowd is everything" says Nigel. "Having a personal number plate with the company name on goes a long way to achieving this," he added.

Nigel says that the number plate was also bought as an investment. Marketing Manager at Regtransfers.co.uk, Len Stout said, "Companies tend to buy personalised number plates with investment in mind so that if they need to raise some cash fairly rapidly, they can sell them without too much trouble. When a number plate is associated with a company, it can often command a higher price than usual because of the exposure it has had. We are very pleased that thousands of our customers come back to us when they want to sell their number plates." *24 September 2001*

Flash Gordon meets Brash Jordan

Believe it or not, the next batch of new style number plates are already being thought up by the UK's leading number plate dealer, Regtransfers.co.uk.

Between 1 and 30 November 2001 the new '02' numbers (replacing the current '51' numbers), became available. Joseph Randlesome, Business Development Manager at Regtransfers.co.uk says, "We have come up with some excellent number plates with the age identifier for March 2002. For instance, JP02 TER (J. PORTER), JG02 DON (J. GORDON), JJ02 DAN (J. JORDAN), WH02 LEY (Whorley) and MO02 TON (Moorton).

The new style '51' plates have been selling extremely well, but if you couldn't find your name then, you will have a good chance this time round.

The new system has given the number plate market a new lease of life with these new combinations, especially with them changing every six months now. The traditional 'cherished' number plates are still as popular as ever, but not everyone can afford them. The new system gives everyone a real opportunity of owning a personalised number plate."

A special page, 'New Style Reg's', has been set up on the Regtransfers website www.regtransfers.co.uk for customers to search for their name, initials, hobby or whatever interesting word they can think of. Drop down menus allow ease of use, so you don't have to remember that you can't use the letters I, Q or Z in the two letters before the '02' or I and Q in the three letters after the '02'."

24 October 2001

N orman Parrish from Warwickshire, considered cherished number plates to be naff, until a friend of his told him he'd seen a number plate with his initials on - NHP 1!

NHP 1 (for Norman Harvey Parrish) is one of the highly sought after 'Number one' style number plates. Norman said, "I've noticed that everyone's got one these days,

any more!

and when my friend saw this number plate I told him I was not going to be tempted. I have always said I would never get a cherished number plate because I think they are so naff!"

Soon after, Norman saw a Rolls Royce Silver Spirit II for sale in his favourite colour - dark blue. "I thought, no, I'm not going to buy it, after all, I already have a Daimler V8. But I kept thinking about the Rolls Royce - I'd always wanted one! I ended up buying the Rolls Royce - then I started to weaken over the number plate! I rang up Regtransfers.co.uk the same day I bought the car, just to see how much NHP 1 cost. It was a lot of money! I thought, this is silly! and decided to sleep on it. I bought NHP 1 the next day."

When asked if he still thinks cherished number plates are naff, Norman replied, "Not so much now! People seem very impressed by the plate, they look to see who I am."

Jim Stewart, who after 11 years with Regtransfers.co.uk, is their longest serving salesman, said: "Mr. Parrish liked the plate so much he came back and bought T1 NHP for his 'T' registration Daimler. When I spoke to him he had definitely resigned himself to the fact that he was about to become the proud owner of a second cherished number plate! It's great when someone is converted like that. In my experience, as soon as people realise the wide range that is available to them, from their initials, a hobby or a nickname, to the more expensive 'number one's', they become dead set on finding the perfect plate for them. My job is to help them find the best possible number plate whilst staying within their price range."

What a shame that Mr. Parrish just missed out on buying the number plate N1 AFF, which has been sold by Regtransfers.co.uk to a man in Essex!

27 September 2001

Surnames served on a plat

Top of the shopping list for many cherished number plate enthusiasts is still the surname plate - it identifies them wherever they go and it is the ultimate accessory for personalising a vehicle.

This was certainly the case for Peter Grey-Hughes, who purchased 6 REY (Grey) in preference to a plate which spells his first name, such as PET 33R or P3 TER. "Grey is my maternal family name and forms part of my own surname. I was not interested in a plate with 'Peter' on it, I only wanted my surname." Peter was looking for a number plate for his second car, a Range Rover, and thought that this plate matched the car perfectly. "I also have the number plate GH 7, which is on a V6 Mercedes. I definitely prefer 6 REY though, and it certainly draws admiring glances. I only need one car now, so I'm selling the Mercedes with the number plate on it. It would be a great plate for Geri Halliwell, Gloria Huniford or Glen Hoddle!"

Barry Tuck who deals with the email sales enquiries at the premier Cherished Number plate dealer, Regtransfers.co.uk said, "I find that people are often both very proud and very defensive of their surnames. I think it defines who we are, and where we come from, whereas a christian name, especially one that is quite ordinary just blends in with the crowd. We all want to be a bit different from everyone else, and buying a personalised number plate is one way people can express their individuality. Mr. Grey-Hughes had seen the plate in one of our adverts and contacted me about it. For him, it was the best possible number plate."

e still a delectable choice

Likewise, Mark Dewey found an excellent number plate to match his surname, D6 WEY. He saw it advertised in one of Regtransfers adverts and said to himself, "I'll have that one!" He had seen DEW 6Y a few years ago, which planted the seed of wanting a personalised number plate with his surname. Mark has his own building/renting business, Tatlif Properties which is based in Lower Broadheath, Worcester. "I received a first class service from a very amiable chap."

John Carr who dealt with the sale said, "Mr. Dewey has found an excellent plate for his unusual surname. He is now looking to add another 'surname' plate to his collection!"

Nick Whale, of Nick Whale Holdings Ltd from Warwickshire, a motor distributor for Toyota, Lexus and Lotus, has also found an excellent number plate to match his surname, W77 ALE. "I received a mail shot from Regtransfers.co.uk and was on the phone to them within the hour. It is good value and an efficient service!"

Three special search facilities have been built into the www.Regtransfers.co.uk website specifically for names: 'Is your name available?', 'Names & Initials' and 'Plates like Names'.

When your details are typed in, all the plates available that match, will appear. If the name you are looking for is not available, you can use the Regtransfers excellent 'Reg Alert' service. Request the plate you are looking for and the results will be emailed to you as they are found.

4 October 2001

Jon Culverhouse, Managing Director of the Luton based company, Fantastic Fireworks, bought a 'bang on' number plate - 5 NOV, to further promote his nationwide business.

"I am always looking for ways to advertise and promote my company, and having a personalised number plate is an excellent way of achieving that. I owned M18 ANG for a while, but wanted a plate that was more obviously connected to bonfire night, so I started to look around for another mark. I was offered 8 ANG (Bang), but I wanted a plate that encapsulated what Fantastic Fireworks is all about. I thought of NOV 5, so I contacted Regtransfers.co.uk. They advised me that this plate had never been issued, but by coincidence 5 NOV had just come onto their books. I was very lucky! It's the sort of plate that will be a collector's item. I was pleasantly surprised at the price as well, I was expecting to pay much more. We use it in our advertising and it has really helped to promote our company. We often get TV crews turning up who want to film me with the car because of the registration mark - the plate really has paid for itself. We have even named our website 5Nov.com! "

Jon's company now supplies very high profile occasions such as the Millennium celebrations, the Big Brother finale (when Craig won), the last night of Wembley Stadium and even the celebrations at Old Trafford when Manchester United won their third concecutive Premiership title.

Fantastic Fireworks next major project is to open a big fireworks outlet at the Moto Toddington Services (Northbound) near Junction 12 of the M1 on October 17. "I'm

going to take the car up there to help to promote this new venture."

The Company's usual customer base ranges from retail, weddings, private parties, corporate events, football matches and larger scale displays, for instance those organised by the council for New Year's eve or Bonfire Night.

The 5th November is like Christmas to us, we are always incredibly busy. A 5-minute display will have taken around 54 hours to plan - from initial consultation through to planning, design, fusing, packing, loading, set-up and execution. With over 16 years experience, we take pride in ensuring that displays are not only spectacular, but safe as well." Safety kit such as barrier tape, helmet, safety goggles, overalls and a safety video can be bought directly from Fantastic Fireworks. Training courses are also available. Many questions such as: Do I need a licence?, Who should I notify?, Where can I hold a display? and What if it rains? are all answered on the Fantastic Fireworks website www.5nov.com

"Since the Millennium celebrations, the popularity of fireworks has rocketed! We are expecting a bumper year." Fantastic Fireworks are finalists in The Daily Telegraph / Energis Customer Services Award. Ironically perhaps, the winner will be announced in November!

25 October 2001

After his phenomenal success with the Ayia Napa hit 'Do You Really Like It?' DJ Pied Piper is celebrating with the purchase of a special number plate for his blue Porsche Carrera 2.

"I wasn't really into personal number plates until a friend of mine, Creed, said to me 'that car needs a private plate'. He owns C7 EED, which is great, but I thought to myself, if I am going to get one I would prefer something more subtle. I saw the number plate 2 DEX (as in 2 Decks) in the Regtransfers sales brochure and the more I thought about it the more I thought that this was the dream plate for me. When I rang back about it, I was gutted when they told me that it had just been sold! By this time I was really hooked on the idea of having a private plate, so I started to look at other options. I didn't want a plate with 'DJ' on it, although I did look for 'Piper', but apparently someone already owns that. I finally decided on 15 EN, which is a very personal choice for me. Only close friends and family know the true meaning behind it."

Pied Piper says he got his DJ name many years ago: "I was in a club, waiting to go on when someone came up to me and asked me what my DJ name was. I didn't have one, so as I had a three hour wait for my turn, I thought I'd better come up with one! Pied Piper just seemed to make sense." In the original verse by Robert Browning,

_uvin' it, Luvin' it, Luvin' it!"

The Pied Piper of Hamelin mesmerised the rats and then the town's children with his music. It has proved a memorable and appropriate name for him, as one enthusiastic fan commented on a website recently: "'Do You Really Like It' has contagious lyrics that make this song the best on the planet!"

DJ Pied Piper and The Master of Ceremonies have a new single 'We are here', out on 10 December 2001. "We are shooting the video for it next week. The album will be out early next year, but we haven't got a name for that yet." D J Pied Piper and the MC's were nominated for three MOBO awards recently including 'Best Single' and 'Best Newcomer'.

To date they have won 'Best Club Anthem' at the UK Garage Awards and 'Best Club Track' (voted by all clubs in the country) amongst others. "The Smash Hits Awards are coming up soon and we will be going on the Smash Hits Tour."

30 October 2001

Buy your loved one a number plate gift voucher this Xmas

Premier Personalised Number Plate Dealer, Regtransfers.co.uk have launched their new gift vouchers just in time for the Christmas rush. A special information page called 'Gift Vouchers' can be found on the website www.regtransfers.co.uk suggesting all the special occasions that may require a very different kind of present for that person in their life who has everything.

There are four voucher options available, £50 (blue), £100 (bronze), £250 (silver) and £500 (gold).

There is no set time in which the vouchers have to be redeemed and they can be used in full or part payment for any number plate purchased from Regtransfers.

The Gift Voucher Scheme has been put together by Regtransfers Marketing Executive, Samantha Baldwin, "I think they will be a very successful gift idea, especially for those people who want to buy someone a number plate, but aren't quite sure which one to buy. We make it an extra special present by supplying a certificate with the vouchers, which can include a personal message from you to your loved one."

18 October 2001

England victory creates historic number plates

A couple from Rotherham, South Yorkshire have bought two number plates to mark England's momentous victory against Germany on Saturday.

EN51 GER (England 5, Germany 1); GB51 GER (GB 5, Germany 1) were purchased by Mr and Mrs Spalding to make up for Mr. Spalding missing the historic game. "My husband is a joiner and he was working at a school. The job needed to be finished before the beginning of term. I taped the game and he watched it on Sunday night, but it wasn't the same, the atmosphere wasn't there. We bought the number plates to make up for the disappointment of missing the live game."

The only other person in the country to think of spelling England's victory on the new style number plates was a man from Surrey, who purchased WE51 WON (We Won 5 -1). Top Salesman, Stuart Henson, at Regtransfers.co.uk, the largest number plate dealer in the UK, sold all three number plates.

"I watched all five goals myself and as soon as these enquiries came through I knew they would be collectors items for the future. Like everyone else, I was delighted with the result. I am sure that these plates will raise a few patriotic smiles!"

20 September 2001

Are you sitting on a goldmine?

When Malcolm Davies purchased his nearly new Silver Fiat Coupe, little did he know that its Northern Ireland number plate would be worth a tidy sum. His 22 year old son and business partner Aaron Davies, also a director of their company in Dunstable, One Stop Van Shop said "When I was looking for a new car, I decided to buy a Fiat Coupe 2 litre because it was the last of that model - they don't make them any more and I think the car will become a classic. I didn't even consider its registration plate TIL 44 until someone pointed out to me that it could be worth something because it is nice and short. We contacted Regtransfers.co.uk to find out and was told that it has a value of around £2,000! We've decided to sell it now and put the money back into the business."

Malcolm Davies started the One Stop Van Shop two years ago when he saw there was a gap in the market. As Van Import Specialists, they guarantee to pass on to their customers the large savings they achieve through their bulk buying power. Malcolm said, "All our vehicles have UK specifications. We offer a total solution by supplying the van, finance, even the accessories - it's a complete service. Customers can expect to save around £7,000 per van. Because we sell different makes, such as Fiat, Ford, Mercedes and Renault, we can give an un-biased opinion about which van will best suit a customers particular needs."

Ruby Speechley, Public Relations Manager at personalised number plate giant Regtransfers.co.uk, said, "This is an excellent find for the Davies', but it is not a completely unusual story. We have had people ring in for a valuation on old vehicles they are about to sell after someone has suggested to them that their plate may be worth something. I have seen a few interesting number plates around town, and I always wonder to myself if the owners realise its potential value. The best one I've seen recently is J4 CKD - which would be perfect for the comedian Jack Dee!"

7 December 2001

Magical Christmas present for Harry Potter

A young Harry Potter look-alike from Luton has found the perfect Christmas present for the magical character he plays in his local theatre. David Pratt, a twelve year old Harry Potter fan was delighted when his Uncle, who works for local number plate company, Regtransfers.co.uk, told him they had purchased his ideal number plate, POT 73R - he couldn't wait to get his hands on it!

"It is such a cool plate, it would be great if Father Christmas could get it for me!" David plays the young magician in the pantomime 'Aladdin' at the Radlett Arts Centre in Hertfordshire. Mum, Beverley said: "David comes on as Harry near the end of the panto, giving the play a quirky ending with a distinctive Harry Potter flavour - the audience love it."

David was upset when he missed the auditions for the part in the hit film Harry Potter and the Philosopher's Stone, but he is keen to find out where the auditions are for the third film, so he can go along. Beverly said, "David is such a massive Potter fan – he's read the books eight times so far! He has been going to acting classes for three years now at Barnfield College in Luton. They do singing, dancing and acting."

David said: "My ambition is to be in an action or adventure film. I would love to play Harry in a West End Theatre, and have the POT 73R plate on my broomstick!"

21 December 2001

This 1951 Allard P1 (36cc) is part of the Stondon Transport Museum Collection. It is one of only 25 examples left in the world today. Sydney Allard actually won the Monte Carlo Rally driving one of these in 1952. Hardly what you'd call pretty but aluminium panelling kept its weight down and performance up.

The P1 was Allard's best seller but its old Ford V8 engine was something of a gas guzzler.

MLW 872 was issued in London in 1951.

Stories

The Stories behind why people choose the number plates that they do, and what they mean to them.

Campbell car and plate back together again

Three years ago, Phillip Haslam from Derbyshire bought and imported a 1933 Aston Martin le Mans from St. Louis, Missouri. Phillip says, "The car was purchased new by Sir Malcolm Campbell shortly after he had taken the World Land Speed Record. Apparently Malcolm Campbell always chose a registration number with the figure '1' in it and he always had his cars painted Bluebird Blue to match his original car.

When the car arrived in England it came complete with the plate ALW 1, but I later discovered that, as the car had been in America since early in the 1960's the number had long since lapsed. Through the DVLA, I discovered that ALW 1 was owned by someone else, but they were not prepared to release any details. At the time I was somewhat disappointed as I was keen that the number should be reunited with the car.

One Sunday, in mid-August, for some unknown reason I happened to glance at the registration numbers in The Sunday Times – for no particular reason whatsoever (I had never really thought of looking for the number previously). Imagine my surprise when the number ALW 1 leapt out of the page at me from in amongst the thousands of numbers that Regtransfers were advertising – it really did seem such incredible fate that the number was available for sale at the one time in my life that I have ever looked at the adverts. Happily now, the car is reunited with its original number."

From enthusiasm to elation!

Who would have thought that five years ago, someone who knew nothing about number plates would get so involved with them to the point that he now owns three? Well that's just what's happened to Len Stout, Registration Transfers Marketing Manager. He joined the company in 1997 to take control of their advertising and move it forward when not long afterwards the bug struck.

Len and his wife Christine treated themselves to L9 VES (Loves) to celebrate their 30th wedding anniversary. Not long afterwards Len was able to acquire S7 OVT, the nearest he ever thought he would get to his ultimate number plate. But, when he least expected it, S7 OUT came onto the books at Regtransfers!

Len could hardly contain himself and with a little encouragement from Christine and his boss Tony (not that it took much anyway), he bought the plate straight away.

"There's nothing like believing your own publicity, is there?", said Len. "And now that I've got something truly special that my wife and I can enjoy for the rest of our lives. We can even pass it down through the family."

Number plate of a lifetime

A very proud North Wales man has secured the number plate of a lifetime in the shape of 9 EY. Mr. Steve Pentith, who runs his own business, Pentith Self-catering Holidays, in Benllech, Anglesey, had been searching for an EY plate for quite some time. "I found the number plate 9 EY on the Regtransfers.co.uk website. I was so pleased to have found an EY plate! About a month after I bought it, another number plate dealer rang me and offered me more money for it, but I would never sell it. I'd like to keep it in the family and pass it down when the time comes."

Steve says that any EY plates are highly sought after in Anglesey, "in fact I often see a blue BMW around town with the number plate EY 9. I've also seen EY100 and 5 EY and my son's neighbour has 3 EY on his Mercedes. I have even parked next to a Mitsubishi Shogun with the plate 8 EY. The reason for this interest is that the very first number plate registered in Anglesey was EY 1, in 1903. It was first acquired by a wealthy land owner. Apparently his chauffeur queued up all night to make sure he secured it. I have done a bit of research into Anglesey plates and have found out that EY 9 was first issued by the council on 17 December 1903 to a Mr. Aiden Henry Williams Llewelin Morgan at the Plas Coed Mor (the Big House). The car it went on was a 9 N.H.P. Darracq 12bhp. Unfortunately a lot of EY number plates have been lost or destroyed, which makes the ones around even more desirable."

Mother finds Bart Simpson plate

Mother of three, Debra Hastings was looking at the Regtransfers website one day when she came across C8 ART. She thought that this looked the perfect number for her eight year old son Bart, and a much more affordable version than 8 ART. "It was a spur of the moment decision.

It is a present for him, for when he is 18. At the moment he hates his name - we let his 16 year old brother, Greg, name him after Bart Simpson, but I am sure he will grow into his name as he gets older."

The Hastings' are now looking for a number plate for their four year old son Jacob. "J4 COB would be nice, but it's probably a bit pricey. We know we'll find a cheaper version, so we'll just keep looking."

Always remembered, never forgotten

John S. Harrington from Gainsborough in Lincolnshire bought the
personal number plate J5 THW as a memorial to his late wife Tina
Harrington-Wells. "Tina sadly died aged 42, two days before Christmas
2000 in Lincoln County Hospital following complications after a routine
operation. We had been married for only five years. The registration
means a great deal to me and will be cherished for the rest of my life."

John originally wanted to buy a number plate with Tina's date of birth,
9 November, but found that the number 911 was very popular amongst
Porsche drivers, and therefore quite rare. "J5 THW was just right, J for
my initial, 5 for the five years we were married and THW for Tina's
initials.
I know she is still around me, I have heard movement in the house. It all
helps to comfort me." The plate is on John's white Mercedes.

Cherished plate for the Irish

"I purchased this number for my initials - M.I.C." says Martin Iain Clayton from County Durham. "Ireland never issued the letters MIC and I didn't want a prefix M even if I could get it, so a suffix C was the only option open to me to get my initials on a registration plate.

I am extremely pleased with my new registration number and make no mistake ANM 1C will be cherished for the rest of my motoring life. I received an exceptionally friendly and helpful service from Regtransfers."

Perfect presie from Grandad

Who could wish for a kinder Grandad than Mr. Ken Ball from the West Midlands who has bought the number plate ASH 13Y for his fifteen year old Grandson, Ashley Roberts. "The idea is to give it to him as a 17th birthday present - especially as he is hoping to pass his driving test that very day!"

Ken says. "He'll have lessons before hand then he'll be ready for the test as soon as he reaches that magical age. It was my daughter Donna's idea, she saw it in the Regtransfers advert in Exchange & Mart and said to me: 'Oh Dad, a plate for Ashley, but I haven't got the money!' It will be a good investment for his future as well." Ken has been into number plates since 1972 and has a couple of his own 27 KB and 47 KB (which is currently for sale).

Surprise retirement present for Gerald

When Gerald Salmon retired last year, his wife Rosina marked the occasion with a surprise present - a personalised number plate of his very own.

T1 GWS was significant to Gerald because it ends with his initials, GWS. "It is on my 'T' Reg car, a Peugeot 306 Meridian (special edition). It was always a whim of mine to own a personal number plate. It was a lovely surprise."

Taking the plunge

Kevin Vine from Hedge End, near Southampton has the 'initials' number plate 468 KV. Kevin says: "Having considered for some time whether or not to purchase a

cherished number plate, I decided to take the plunge upon seeing this plate for sale in a Regtransfers advertisement. The plate now sits proudly on my Ford Probe and I shall be on the look out for plates for my children in the near future.

Thank you to Regtransfers for your help in a smooth transition of my acquisition."

And so to bed

The perfect name for the perfect bed company. Patrick Clacy's business in the centre of Oxford supplies the highest quality brass, iron and wooden beds in the country. As a branch of the London based store, they are renowned as hand made bed specialists.

Patrick Clacy recently decided to purchase a new van for his business and said "I needed a number plate to finish off the look of the van. I thought that CO51 BED was a fun number plate and would be noticed as it is out delivering all over the country. I think it will help to make us stick in people's minds when they see the company name and then the number plate on the van when it is out and about.

It would also be nice if it holds its value or even increases in value, but it's not the reason I bought it." Patrick has already purchased 4554 SC for his wife, Sandra Clacy.

Perfect plate purchase celebrates lucky win

Winning a car in a competition would be a dream come true for many people, but then finding your perfect number plate to go with it, has to be out of this world!

Paula Jacklin from Buckinghamshire won a Ford Ka in a competition sponsored by Alders Department Stores. "I wanted my own personalised number plate to go with it. I like to stand out in a crowd - subtly though, not in your face, so I chose M15 PDJ - it looks like Miss PDJ which are my initials. I have had the plate on my MX-5 and because it is a 'W' registration, many people realise that it is a private plate because an 'M' registration Mazda MX-5 would have the groovy pop up lights. Although I opted for a subtle choice of plate, if I had the money I would be seriously tempted by P4 ULA, which apparently is back on the market with Regtransfers.co.uk."

Tribute and memorial to late wife

"D1 KRB was found purely by chance whilst one of my colleagues was looking on the Regtransfers website" says Mr. Keith Raymond Banks from Rugeley, Staffs.

"I felt that I must buy this registration as a tribute and memorial to my late wife of 37 years, Doreen Iris, who passed away in June of this year."

Record number plate

Brian Davies of Gwynedd, Wales, thought that the number plate COB 1K was a great way to publicise his company COB Records.

"I am now looking for another plate with 'COB' to match it" he said.

Mr. Bean buys a number plate for his wife

Nigel Bean from Bedale, North Yorkshire had always fancied a cherished plate. His ideal plate would have been N8 EAN.

When he looked into purchasing this it wasn't available, however C8 EAN was, so he decided to buy it as an anniversary gift for his wife Claire. He is now keeping an eye out for H8 EAN for their son Harry.

Mad about Derby

Paul Sisson from Oakwood in Derby has found a number plate he can cherish forever, D3 RBY. "I chose D3 RBY because Derby is the place of my birth, I'm proud of the city and I'm mad about Derby County Football Club." Paul logged on to Regtransfers.co.uk and used their search facilities to find this appropriate number. "My number plate looks fantastic on my new Jag!"

A dream car and a plate to go with it

Recently retired Des Yeates from Aylburton, near Lydney in Gloucestershire, is proud of his new car and personalised number plate, P200 DES.

It was due to his wife wanting him to sell up his motorbike and 'get four wheels' that Des decided that now was the right time: "It has been my cherished ambition for many years to have my own dream car - an MGF with its own number plate - and lo and behold it's come to fruition. It is a wonderful retirement present from me to me! A local person recommended Regtransfers.co.uk to me and that is how I was able to realise my dream."

On your bike! - D8 FFY ducks out of new style numbers

While the rush is on to find the best of the new style number plates, Mr. Daffyd Lowery ('Daffy') from Hillingdon, Middlesex, is buying up old style number plates as an investment. "The time to buy the old plates is now. With the introduction of the new combinations, the old style plates are sure to go up in value, especially a great plate like D8 FFY," he said.

Mr. Lowery owns a Classic Motorcycle shop on the Uxbridge Road, but he says he started out on his parents egg farm in Lincolnshire many years ago, "They got me on to the whole plate thing, I remember they had the number plates EGG 4T and EGG 25 which they sold on to 'Thames Valley Eggs.'" Two of the other plates Mr. Lowery owns are C10 FFY and M11 AGU, which he is selling. "M11 AGU is on an MV Augusta F4 S Motorbike - a great choice for the enthusiast." When we bought the MV Augusta, it came with the number plate A6 UMV which is good as well."

"Mr. Lowery told me that he is known as Daffy and that he'd had his eye on the D8 FFY plate for sometime", says Tim Wheatley, the sales person at Regtransfers.co.uk who dealt with Mr. Lowery's call. "He told me that he drives a hard bargain, but that he couldn't resist this plate any longer! Mr. Lowery is among

a growing number of shrewd business people who are buying number plates and selling them on, we've even had Building Society and Bank managers purchasing plates as an investment."

Although Mr. Lowery's preference is the old style plates, people are also buying the new style number plates as an investment - they think of good words or names, buy them up early and then sell them on. For example, Mr. Nazir from Birmingham purchased DE51 GNA (designer) and BE51 DEU (beside you) amongst others, before September 1st when the new style plates first came out. He said, "I looked up in the dictionary for words you could make with the 51 age identifier. I also thought of DE51 REU (desire you) and DE51 DEU (decide you). With the new '02's' available right through November, it's a great time to put your thinking cap on.

Celebration on a plate

Geoff and Barbara Welsh from Cheshire are celebrating the purchase of their new number plate G8 WEL. "As we are Geoff and Barbara Welsh, we feel it now assumes the names of GB WELSH!"

"My husband is 43 years old and I am 61. We have been married for 13 years and love fast cars. The 'three' of us look great together. We are so happy to have found Regtransfers.co.uk on the internet. Thank you to Jayne Simmonds for her kind and helpful advice at the time."

Plate joke wearing thin!

Jennifer Samuel from Holyport in Berkshire received R30 JEN as a gift from her husband a couple of years ago. Jennifer said: "My husband was always on about getting me a personalised number plate ever since he got one for his car a few years ago. When I bought an R reg car in 2000, his first thought was to get me a new plate for it.

Looking through the available ones, we could not decide on whether we should get one with my initials JKS or JEN, short for Jennifer. When the final choice came to R30 or R40 JEN we decided to go for R30 since we had been married almost 30 years (in June 2002). The only reaction I get (apart from people wanting to know why I have one in the first place) is from people in garages. When I go to pay for petrol they say "Thank you, Jen" or "Hello, Jen". I must admit it get a bit wearing at times – a joke lasts only so long!"

Mastiffs deserve their own plate

Christine Ballardie says that they chose the number plate 21 KTM for their Khukli Tibetan Mastiffs. "We picked a car suitable to convey our dogs so thought it only right and proper that they should have their own number plate.

At present we have a family of 10 Tibetan Mastiffs living with us in our home and can only hope that the 21 does NOT represent our final number!"

Bit of a Devil!

Ken Madigan from Kirkby in Liverpool has a devil of a number plate – 666 KM. Ken said: "It is a very apt number plate because I have always been told throughout my life that I am a bit of a devil! It also has my initials KM.

The service that Regtransfers provided was second to none."

A truly scumptious number plate!

Tony Green, from Lancashire has built his own Truly Scrumptious replica of the Chitty Chitty Bang Bang car, under licenced agreement with MGM. For the finishing touch, Tony turned to Regtransfers for a GEN (short for genie) number plate. Tony was delighted when he found GEN 22.

"I remember seeing the film in 1968 and it had a big influence on me at the time. I still think today that it has all the right 'ingredients' to entertain generations to come. I was showing my Chitty memorabilia at various exhibitions around the UK and people kept asking me if I owned the original car. I hated having to say no, so when someone said to me 'You have the plans why don't you build one?' I thought I would! The car has taken me 2 years to build (evenings and weekends). I have used the original plans

and the original film car builder has finished the planking to the boat section for me. But it wouldn't be the same without a GEN number plate. The plate GEN 11 is famously assigned to the original car, so when I found GEN 22 I was more than pleased! Now the car is complete, I will be exhibiting it around the country".

Good investment for all the family

Ivan Scott, from Burnley in Lancashire, is pushing his hobby of collecting personalised number plates beyond just buying them for fun, he is now buying and selling them with investment firmly in mind. For instance, he waited 17 years before he had the chance to buy his ultimate plate - 1 VY (Ivy is his nickname), but 18 months later he had an offer for it that he just felt he couldn't turn down, so he sold it again!

More recently Ivan has bought 11 YS for his daughter Yasmin's eleventh birthday. "She is delighted with the present. The plate is currently on our Citroen people carrier, but of course it will stay with her for as long as she wants it."

Ivan currently has OVA 1 on his Mercedes, which is an excellent plate for anyone interested in cricket, and he has 3 VN on his BMW. "I enjoy seeing the number plates on my cars, it makes them look special and personalises the car, making it stand out from all the rest. Stuart Henson, the salesman at Regtransfers.co.uk has given me some great advice on what to buy, I am very grateful to him."

A runaway success!

Iwan Thomas, Gold Medallist 400M runner has found a runaway number plate that no competition will be able to keep up with! - R400 RUN. "It's a great way to celebrate my wins, and it's such an appropriate number plate for me."

Athletics wasn't always for Iwan though, from the age of 8, he spent seven very successful years in BMX biking - coming 2nd, 4th and 9th in National and World BMX Championships. But it has been in athletics that Iwan has excelled - setting a new British Record of 44.36 seconds in 1997.

In 1998, Iwan went on to win a Gold medal in the Commonwealth Games, two Gold medals in the European Championships and the World Cup. Of the various awards Iwan has received, the MBE awarded to him in 1999 was probably his most prestigious to date.

From PO51 BLY the best number plate company in the World!

It was a process of elimination for Peter Doherty of Hayes, Middlesex when it came to choosing a new number plate for his Mercedes CLK230 Convertible.

The Project Manager decided to 'Ask Jeeves' to find a plate that spelt a word. "I used their crossword to come up with a list of 12 or more words." As Peter is an Architect by trade, he was initially looking for DE51 GNS, DE51 RED or DE51 RES but was disappointed to find that they had already been sold. "It came up with ones like MU51 CTV and MU51 CMD, which would be great plates, but they too had gone. Someone suggested DY51 XYA (Dyslexia spelt incorrectly). They rang the DVLA out of curiosity but were told that it wouldn't be released in case it offended someone. We were quite surprised really, considering some of the 'naughty plates' they have released."

Peter had never thought of buying a personalised number plate until he decided to buy a new car. He has decided to sell PO51 BLY through Regtransfers.co.uk, where he first purchased it. He is looking to buy other plates that spell words, as an investment.

Famous plate BS 1 is coming home

BS 1 has changed hands after almost thirty years. It was owned by Billy Smart (Junior) of circus fame since 1972 and has now been transferred through number plate dealer Regtransfers.co.uk to Bill Spence of Kirkwall in Orkney to celebrate his firm's centenary. It is also, of course, Bill's initials.

Bill said: "Not only is the plate to mark 100 years of my Shipbroking and Stevedoring Company John Jolly but also, I am glad to say, BS 1 is finally coming home to Orkney where it was first registered on 15 March 1904. I put it on my Jaguar XK8 on its 98th birthday this year and then looked through the old Orkney records in the Kirkwall Archive to establish its provenance. It was originally assigned to William MacLennan of Grainbank who held the registration for 8 years until 1912 when John McEwan, Rector of Kirkwall Grammar School, obtained it. Subsequently it was assigned to the Manager of the National Bank in Kirkwall, George Drever. Then in 1921 Charles Haydon of Lynnfield put the number on his new Crossley. Eight years later the number was in Victoria Street, Stromness when the car was owned by

John Robert Cursiter; then, in early 1930 the Crossley bearing BS 1 was sold to John M. F. Groat of Moasound, Longhope. I first saw BS 1 on the old Crossley in JMF's coal store in the 1950's soon before it left Orkney to go to Sheffield where it was allocated to Bob Stanley."

Bill discovered in the Orkney records that BS 3 was actually the first number registered in Orkney on 21 January 1904. He also found out that the author, George Bernard Shaw was allocated BS 73 on 5 November 1908 and that the motorcycle champion Barry Sheen had BS 7 at one time. Bill himself already owns BS 15, BS 38, BS 43, BS 47 and BS 4747 and his late wife Margaret's grandfather owned BS 14.

"For BS 1's 100th birthday in 2004 I'd like to trace the owners of old cherished BS numbers – authentic ones that were issued originally. I would like to hold a reunion in Orkney during the springtime of 2004 – perhaps around the week preceding 15 March - and have the owners with their cars come to Orkney for a weekend of fun and maybe have a group photo taken of us all with our old plates. It could be a memorable event". Drop Bill Spence a note at P.O. Box 2, KIRKWALL, Orkney, KW15 1HR if you would like to attend.

BS 1 - Bill Spence and AS 1 - Angus Sinclair Alton House, Kirkwall, Orkney.

R6 GER achieves his personal goal after 30 years

Roger Campbell certainly knows how to get noticed - wearing his excellent name plate R6 GER on a smart BMW 728i. "When I decided to purchase a personalised number plate, I initially wanted R6 GER, R8 GER or R9 GER, but none of them were available. Then I considered one with my initials 'RC', but they were too expensive. Then Regtransfers said that R6 GER had become available - I had to have it!"

Roger's interest in number plates started some 30 years ago when he saw an immaculate black Transit Van in London. "It had gold lettering down the sides spelling 'Chanel', then to my amazement I noticed that the number plate was 'NO 5'." After this, Roger was well and truly hooked, and for years always wanted his own, 'RAC 1'. Knowing this would be near impossible to locate let alone afford, he decided that moment to set himself a personal goal, which he would have to wait nearly 30 years to achieve. Thanks to Regtransfers "excellent, first class service", his dream has finally been realised.

Roger's company, Westbury Carpets & Floor Coverings in Milton Keynes celebrated 25 years in business in May 2002. It's continued success is due to Roger's high personal motivation and his determination to deliver 100% customer satisfaction.

A plate in loving memory

How do you get over the shock of your beloved husband dying suddenly? Perhaps you never can, but Nichola Dix has found an unusual way to ease the pain.

She has purchased a number plate with her husbands name on, N100 BOB. "The N is for Nichola, and 100 signifies the score in darts, as Bob used to love to play in the old days, along with many other sports. He was cruelly taken from me aged only 56. The number plate gives me such comfort, I can't tell you. I come out of work and it's like he is there waiting for me."

The idea for buying a number plate came to Nichola the day before his funeral. "I decided to get the number plate BOB 1 made up, just to lay in his coffin. He'd often thought about having a 'posey' plate. Soon after, I decided to buy one for real, in his memory."

Bob Dix was a Divisional Fire Officer, risking his life every day. He played in the squad of the National Fire Service football team representing England in his early youth, and later becoming treasurer. Now every year a trophy in his memory is presented at the National Fire Service Cup Final. Bob was also a National Fire Service fishing champion, which covers Fire Service fishermen from England, Scotland and Wales. Bob won many fishing trophies over the years. A special trophy is now awarded each year in his memory, for the heaviest fish caught at the National Fire Service fishing competition in Ireland.

"He is greatly missed by everyone. He was a very fair man, with a vibrant personality. Our sons and I miss him terribly. I know I can't bring him back, but at least when I am driving my car it is as though he is still with me."

Rottweilers snap up plates

Jerry and Rosita Howell have found a suitable plate for their two Rottweilers – R8 ROT. Jerry said: "The dog on the left in the photo is 'Royce' (kennel club name "Samals Reasonable Force") and the dog on the right is called "Bentley" (kennel club name "Samals Soul Legend"). We show both the dogs and have shown Bentley at Crufts. We chose the plate for obvious reasons and R8 ROT was the shortest we saw. When we don't do so well at shows we often think of the registration as irate rot!

When we first got the plate we did not see any others around, but I think we started a trend as there's a few now but not as cool as ours. We have three children as well as the dogs who all get on very well. It's a shame they have such a bad reputation as they are very loveable cuddly bears really, as long as you're not a burglar!! We have also recently purchased RO51 TAS from Regtransfers for Rosita. She is now the envy of all her friends."

Willie Carson backs a winner!

Breeder, broadcaster and former champion jockey Willie Carson will no longer have any problem recognising his Isuzu Trooper in a field of 4x4s now that he has added his own special personalised number plate to the vehicle.

Willie, who always stands out in a crowd thanks to his bubbly personality, *but not height* turned to Regtransfers.co.uk to customise his vehicle. Willie was looking for a particular plate he had seen in one of their adverts, which appear in the national newspapers every week. "I telephoned Regtransfers about a plate I was after, but one of Regtransfers excellent sales people, Jim Stewart, found a far more appropriate plate for me."

Jim Stewart said, "As a former 'number one' champion jockey, I thought an N1 plate would be in keeping with Willie's status." Coupled with his initials to make the plate, N1 WHC, it's no wonder Willie changed his mind!

Benign plates join MGB

Ivor Griffiths from Ashley, Hants likes to add the personal touch to his cars by adding cherished registrations. Ivor said: "My 1979 MGB GT was something special. It had 28,000 miles on the clock from new and was in original mint condition - it had not needed any restoration work. When I bought this car I felt that it needed something adding to it to indicate my feelings for the car and the only thing I could think of was a special personal registration plate. I was fortunate to be able to source MGB 1P. The cherished number and the condition of the car brings many admiring glances as I drive it around the New Forest in Hampshire.

A cherished registration is something which I like to have on a vehicle, it adds that personal touch. To this end my wife, Lesley and I have cherished plates on each of our current vehicles. They are both B9 numbers. The B9 represents the word benign which is shown in the dictionary as meaning gracious, gentle, etc. I have B91 VOR, depicting my forename and Lesley has B9 LPG, depicting her initials."

Arsenal plates - a definite winner

The UK's leading number plate dealer, Regtransfers.co.uk have produced an amazing hat trick for any Gunner looking to adorn his car and show his allegiance to the London club with - AR51 NAL, AR51 NEL and AR51 NHL.

AR51 NAL has already been purchased by a private buyer, but the other plates could be snapped up by the team to add the finishing touch to their club coach as they drive around the country. Or perhaps one of it's high profile players could be interested. "They are classic plates whoever purchases them and are definitely a sound investment."

A plate set in stone

A company called Heritage 2000, a stonework restoration business based in Carmarthenshire, Wales, has an added extra on its company vans - personalised number plates - H20 OOA and H20 OOS. Mr. Douglas Somerfield, who owns the company, said: "The plates have helped enormously to advertise the company, which was the original purpose of buying them. We've even got a phone number which ends with 2000 now!"

Heritage 2000 specialise in restoring castles, churches and historic buildings in England and Wales. The company was established 16 years ago. "The year 2000 was definitely our year, and the plates have helped to give us a big impact."

Plate is perfect for advertising

What better way to advertise your own company, than buying a personalised number plate that stands for your company name as well as your own initials. Mr. John Graham Bouch purchased S55 JGB for his company, Steriliser Sales-Service. "The fives look like S's, and my initials are J.G.B, so this plate was perfect. It has really helped to advertise my company, especially as I've also got what it stands for printed at the bottom of the plate. It also helps me when I'm parking in a private or NHS hospital - I don't get clamped because I leave a note on my dashboard saying who I am and why I'm there, and the plate confirms this." Mr. Bouch's company sterilises instruments for Doctors, Dentists, hospitals, tattoo bars, acupuncture clinics and vets. The number plate is on his Mercedes 'A' Class. He is now considering buying a number plate for his wife.

Electrician turned on by number plates

At the age of 10, Keith Butler knew that number plates would become a part of his life. He had been totally fascinated by the number plate 666 HOT on the car of a family friend. "When I saw it, something just clicked, and I was hooked."

Keith's interest was fuelled again years later when he saw Jimmy Tarbuck's famous plate COM 1C in a newspaper article.

In 1987, Keith started KMK of Luton, Bedfordshire, providing electrical and mechanical contract services. One of his earliest personal rewards, needless to say, was to purchase his first cherished number plate H1 KRB (which are his initials). Sheer hard work and endeavour resulted in a substantial ongoing contract that was secured with two large pharmaceutical companies. This success allowed Keith to make another purchase, this time K13 KMK, which represents his company's initials.

KMK continued to thrive with new contracts involving the refurbishment of the Nat-West Tower (after it was bombed) and the 'City Point' project at Moorgate. Keith's ambition of owning his ultimate 'number one' cherished registration drew ever nearer. Two more substantial contracts followed. One was for the MoD and the other for building management services on two of the new Jubilee Line Stations. Their success finally allowed Keith to go for his ideal plate - 1 KRB.

Number 1 KEG seller in the UK

It was whilst he was sitting in his hospital bed, that Alan Morrow saw a personalised number plate that was just right for him - 1 KEG. "It was one of those life changing moments. When I saw it advertised in the Sunday Times, it just struck a cord. My brother already has the number plate A1 KEG, so I suppose the idea had been in the back of my mind."

Morrow Brothers Limited based in Chorley, Lancashire, is the largest seller of stainless steel beer kegs in the UK. "When I roll up at a brewery, it brings a smile to everyone's faces." The number plate is currently on his Jaguar XJR.

Birthday plate
- an eye-catching reminder

John Netting, from Torpoint in Cornwall, was looking for a number plate with a very special date. Having just had his family tree worked out, he discovered that his ancestor, also called John Netting, married a woman called Mary in St. Mellion in 1604. "I was looking for a number plate with the initials J.N. and the date 1604 in memory of this event in my family's history."

"My wife then saw 1609 JN, which signifies my birthday - 16 September, together with my initials. I thought it would be a good one to get as it ensures that none of my friends ever forget my birthday!"

The number plate is on John's Opal Astra, which has his business advertised on it - 'Commercial & Domestic Electrical Installations'. "It has proved very useful for my business, it's a real eye-catcher!"

Body builder worked out B19 PEC

Fitness Base owner, Adrian Howell from Pontefract, West Yorkshire, wanted a personal number plate from a young age. When he rang Regtransfers, the sales woman, Justine suggested B19 PEC to him because he enjoys body building. "I originally wanted a plate with my name on it, but Justine knew that 'Rhino' from Gladiators had the plate B19 PEX, so she was determined to find something similar for me. When she found B19 PEC, she really hit the jackpot. I think it is much better than B19 PEX."

Adrian has been a body builder for around fourteen years now. Six years ago he started to work at Fitness Base when it had only been open for four years, then he bought the gym two years ago. "Everyone knows of Fitness Base around here, and the number plate helps to attract attention."

B16 mark for big dogs

Mrs Sian Spicer couldn't believe her eyes when she saw the plate B16 PYR - she just had to buy it for the family's two Pyrenean Mountain Dogs. "As you can see in the photo, they are not exactly small dogs! This plate suits them well. It looks good on our 13 year old Peugeot 205, which has transported our big boy 'Charlie' around for the past six and a half years, and the other one, 'Little Georgina' for the past eighteen months. They are both thrilled with their number plate!"

Tall woman seeks B16 Plate

Elaine Clark was looking for a number plate that would say something about her to make it completely unique. So when she spotted B16 EMC, she knew that this was the plate for her. "I decided on this number plate because I am 6 foot 1 inch tall and my initials are EMC, so this plate is perfect for me! It looks great on my Shogun."

Good investment for Jimmy

James Harwood from the North West was looking for a number plate for quite some time and decided to use the Regtransfers 'Reg Alert' service to help him. James said: "It wasn't long before I got an email from the reg alert service telling me that J12 MMY was available. This was just what I wanted, so I phoned up straight away to secure it. I had wanted a personal registration for quite a while because it disguises the age of your car. I also wanted a good plate as an investment opportunity. I know that name plates are always a good choice for this because they are so desirable."

Lucky 13 on a plate

Edwin Fry purchased NEF 13 to go on his H registration Jaguar XJS Convertible. "It's my holiday car and has never seen rain. It has only done 13,000 miles and I keep it in an air tent. NEF 13 was purchased to go with my other number, NEF 25. The letters are my initials and 13 is my lucky number. My son, George Hawes Fry has the number GHF 13, which are his initials. The plate is on his Mercedes 230 Kompressor. My other son, Jamie Scott Fry has at present J5 FRY on a BMW 3 series but is willing to sell this registration if he is lucky enough to get JSF 13."

Zippy Mini

Geraldine Smith purchased an old style Mini Cooper recently, and decided that it would be a good idea to get a personalised number plate to go with it. "We thought through what sort of plate we could get - something with a bit of zip in it, like the car, nippy or zippy. The very next day, I saw 21 PPY advertised in one of Regtransfers adverts and had to have it!"

Beatles number plate has hidden message

Pete Gent from St. Albans in Hertfordshire came across a very famous car standing in a car showroom forecourt one day. The car was the white VW Beetle featured on arguably the most famous Beatle's album cover, Abbey Road.

Pete promply bought it, realising that the car salesman had no idea of the history of the car or the plate. "The car became famous largely because of its number plate LMW 281F. A 'Paul is Dead' rumour began on an American radio station with the letters LMW taken as standing for Linda McCartney, widow, whilst 28 IF was widely regarded as a 'clue' that Paul McCartney would have been 28 'IF' he had lived. The fact that McCartney was 27 when Abbey Road was released was conveniently ignored. "I sold the number plate at a Sotherby's auction in 1986 for £2,300. It went to America, but it is now reportedly at the VW factory in Germany. I was hoping to get more for it at the time, but there were only two people bidding. I should have kept it really, but I didn't realise that their popularity would grow again. It would have been great publicity for my guitar shop 'The Music Dept.' "

Parker finds plate for his lady's pink Mercedes

Stan Parker found the plate 41 KNP for his wife Karolyn's pink Mercedes. Stan said: "Driving about in her personalised chariot has given Karolyn a great deal of pleasure. In addition to this it has effectively disguised the true age of the car. Karolyn chose the car for its unique colour 'rosewood'."

Stan says he was very pleased to receive a Volvo and the number plate 8039 SP from Karolyn as a retirement present. "My initials are SP and this was the only plate we could find with these letters. I was very impressed with the service we received from Regtransfers."

Extra special plate

Elaine Clark was looking for a number plate with her initials ECC (Elaine Christine Clark) for some time and decided to use 'Reg Alert', the Regtransfers 'email back' service, (an email is sent to you with details of a number plate that matches your criteria as soon as it comes onto the market). "I hadn't looked for a while, but I received an email from Regtransfers.co.uk. with a £50 discount voucher attached. When I went back to their website, ECC 771 was there, a perfect birthday present for my husband to buy me!"

The car Elaine has put the plate on is a 2 litre Ford Mondeo. "I'm looking for something a bit sportier now. I get lots of comments about the plates; people ask me if they cost a lot. Apparently ECC letters are quite unusual. I was also told that 'ECC' plates were issued in 1956, which is also the year of my birth! It really makes the plates extra special to me."

Scottish farmer's plate double

A farmer from West Kilbride has bought his wife a number plate to match her Scottish name Una. "She had wanted one for quite a while. We saw J1 UNA and thought it looked great. Una is so pleased with it. I also bought L1 EEC (European Economic Community) from Regtransfers as I thought it was a good plate for a farmer! I have now given that to our daughter Vivienne, because her and her husband are also farmers in Carnoustie on the east coast. She absolutely loves it. I am now looking for one which combines my initials and the name of our farm, Chapelton Mains Farm."

Speed or Economy?

Instead of the more conventional name or initials number plate, Bob Woodward came up with an idea that will be envied by boy racers and the like everywhere. It is twenty seven years since Bob had the forethought to purchase 100 MPG (100 miles per gallon), and recently found 'a splendid partner' for it - J100 MPH (100 miles per hour) for his wife Judy. "The J can also stand for James, my son's name, although he is hoping that I will leave 100 MPG to him! J100 MPH is currently on Judy's Ford Ka, whilst 100 MPG is on my red BMW 3.5."

Johnston dynasty on a plate!

Alan Johnston from County Down bought the number plate D111 ACJ from Regtransfers because ACJ are his initials. Alan said: "When I saw the number for sale I had to buy it. For a joke I tell people that I am of the third dynasty of the Johnston family who were engaged in the Irish Linen Industry!"

"I have friends who have IA 1, IA 2 and IA 3 which were the first three numbers ever registered in County Antrim and who inherited these from the late Sir Milne Barbour who was the Grandfather of my friend's wife."

Alan's keen interest in number plates has led him to follow what is sold at auction. "The number OIL 1 was sold last year at auction to a County Fermanagh garage proprietor for over £20,000 and he is hoping to resell it to an Arab Sheik for considerably more!"

A posy of personalised plates

A long established business in Oundle, North Peterborough, has had the edge over its competitors for a while now in the shape of three personalised number plates. J.W. Norman & Son, High Class Fruiterer and Florist, has the plates: M1 JWN, L1 JWN and H1 JWN on its three vans. Mr. James William Norman began the business with his father, back in 1948. 53 years later, he says they are looking forward to the fourth generation of the family joining them. Mr. Norman currently runs the business with his son and daughter.

"We've certainly had a few comments about the plates over the years. It's definitely been worth having them, it lifts you above the herd doesn't it?"

Plate treble for John Smith

For some years Mr. John J. R. Smith from Evesham in Worcestershire had the number plate J888 JRS on his Honda Accord 2.2i Saloon. Recently Regtransfers had J444 JRS for sale and John decided to buy it for his smaller car, a Renault Megane convertible, to make 'a nice pair'.

"When I upgraded my Accord to the 3.0iVTEC V6 Coupe I thought it merited a dateless plate and although a lot more expensive, I bought JRS 789 - 3 initials followed by 3 consecutive numbers. This balanced plate looks great and enhances my new car. J888 JRS has now been relegated to a retention certificate for the time being."

Rolls Royce enthusiasts
cherished number

A Chimney Sweep from Market Weighton in Yorkshire has purchased a plate with
both his and his wife's initials. MKR 872 stands for Mike and Kath Rudd, a simple
but touching statement of their closeness. "We do everything together. Five years ago
we joined the Rolls Royce Enthusiasts Club who found us a 1977 cream coloured
Silver Shadow II Saloon. We go to the club meets every month and the National
Rally, held in Northampton. Like many of the enthusiasts, we are ordinary working
class people who have aspired to owning a Rolls Royce as our hobby."

The Rolls Royce Silver Shadow II Saloon first came out in 1965. It was the first
modern car without a chassis, and had many added extras that we take for granted
today, such as automatic air conditioning and central locking.

"I never really wanted a personalised number plate, until a friend of ours said to us:
'Your car could do with a plate'. We saw this one and thought the initial combination
was just what we wanted. It also has the advantage of making the car look dateless."

'L' plate not enough for Derek

Driving Instructor, Derek Hambly has a plate on his training
car other than the compulsory 'L' plate. He recently purchased
a personalised number plate with his initials - DJH 184. His
driving school takes his name, which means that the plate is
also a good advert for his company. "I often scanned through
the adverts to see if there was a plate with my initials, and was
pleased when this one came up. I wasn't very keen on having a
plate with a letter and number at the beginning. I really wanted
my three initials first and then a number because it makes the
car look dateless. I am very pleased with my purchase!"

Birthday gift plate for business man

Colin Salisbury from Hailsham in East Sussex was very pleased to receive a personalised number plate for his 60th birthday from his wife, Margaret. "CRV stands for my three christian names, Colin Robert Vernon. P8 CRV is currently on my Jaguar Sovereign."

Colin runs several businesses, 'Salisbury Posters' and 'Illuminated Displays Ltd' amongst them. "I may now consider investing in another number plate for one of the business vehicles, especially as we've just purchased a new van. Two of our business cars already have personalised plates."

Partnership with plate for almost 30 years

John Black from Huddersfield has owned the number 1000 CX for almost 30 years. John said: "It caught my eye in a Sunday newspaper advert just at a time when I was looking for a suitable registration to purchase. It immediately appealed to me because it was a 'local' (i.e. Huddersfield) registration, with a nice round number. In fact it is the first reversed Huddersfield number – after YVH 999 had been issued, the local authority started reversed issues at 1000 CX, because 001-999 CX had been allocated for Trade Plates."

John says that 1000 CX has been on seven separate Citroens, most appropriately on three successive Citroen CX's. A Xantia currently bears the registration. "Reversed CX numbers are very rare – only 164 were issued, most of which have probably been scrapped by now.
I would be very pleased to hear from anyone else who owns (or knows of) any other reversed CX registrations."

Jaguar plate for a V12

Terence Garcia from East Sussex bought the plate XJS 12 for his Jaguar XJS, which is a V12. "I had ideally wanted V12 XJS, but it wasn't available, but this is just as good. Trouble is I am thinking of selling the car now and getting something else, so I will be selling the plate as well. The plate is definitely worth a lot more than the car!"

40 years together

On 15th August 1962, Stavros Galanos was issued the number plate 5 DCY by Swansea County Council. Stavros said: "It was for my newly purchased Grecian white Vauxhall VX 4/90. Since then the plate has been on a total of six Vauxhalls, 1 Peugeot 504 ti and now it is on my Rover 75. I have owned this registration number for 40 years this year." Stavros is pictured here with his partner Avril James.

PEPSI challenge for Leicestershire couple

Clifford and Glenice Pepper from Swannington in Leicestershire have found a pair of plates that distinguish them wherever they go. PEP 5Y and P6 PSY could make the famous drinks giant PEPSI, fizz with envy.

Glenice said, "We saw PEP 5Y a long time ago, but by the time we had decided to buy it had gone so we bought P6 PSY instead. Then PEP 5Y came back on the market, so we snapped it up. It is pure self-indulgence really, but we love the plates because of our surname. PEP 5Y is on our Ford Focus and P6 PSY is on the Mercedes SLK."

Higham Disco DJ

Gavin Lancaster 'The Captain' - a professional DJ from Hartlepool wanted the number plate H14 MDJ for several months before he discovered Regtransfers.co.uk. "I was so pleased when I contacted RT and they told me they had this number. It has two meanings for me, firstly it looks like my company name Higham discos and secondly it looks like 'I am DJ'."

"I've had the plate nearly three years now and the reactions I get are excellent. I want to thank Regtransfers for having this registration available on the day I telephoned – it is now on its third car and is almost as well known as I am in Hartlepool. It has been one of the best things I have bought in my 22 years."

Replacement for long lost number

Mike Longton from Surrey says that he has been
interested in cherished numbers since about the 60's:
"I first had a cherished number way back in about 1961
when I bought a Triumph Herald Convertible from
Spikins of Twickenham where a friend of mine was
Stores Manager. He suggested that I write to Middlesex
County Council as they used ML and EML as their
numbers and ask them if they had one available. In those
days it only cost £5 for a number. This I did and was
allocated EML 154. I transferred this number to an Austin
Mini in 1979 but my eldest son wrote it off in 1981 and
due to a misunderstanding with the breaker's yard, I lost
the number."

Mike became interested again recently and was looking
through the number plate adverts in the newspapers when
he saw a relevant number advertised with Regtransfers.
"I contacted Regtransfers but the cost of the number
was too high, however the salesman asked my price
limit and was able to offer H11 EML for my car and I
accepted this."

Plate passed down the family line

63 HHW was owned by Herbert Hayward-Wills but now it has been passed down to his Grandson Adrian Hayward-Wills. Adrian, a Registration Numbers Club member said: "It is on my Ford KA in Derbyshire, where we live. My wife has a matching plate, G3 HHW.

I am hoping my newborn daughter Alice Megan will be able to inherit the plates in years to come. Alice is pictured with the cars after arriving back home for the first time from the hospital. It is perhaps interesting to note that the number plates on both cars are currently taller than her!"

Inside leg measurement on a plate!

Malcolm Eric Oliver was pleased when he purchased a plate with his initials, MEO 32, from Regtransfers. "There is no particular significance to number 32 except it was my age (once!) For a while it was my waist measurement and since about the age of twenty that number has been identified with my inside leg measurement! The smaller the number, the higher the price and I did have my limit."

Plate to go with birthday car

Dairy retailer, John Ball from Cheswardine in Shropshire was delighted to receive a personalised number plate C106 JON for his 50th birthday from his wife. "It is just what I wanted to go with my other birthday present - a yellow Fiat Coupe. I have been looking for a plate for my business, Chipnall Dairy. I haven't managed to find a suitable one yet, but I'm still looking."

Max waves bye bye to MB 1

Max Bygraves, entertainer, sold his beloved MB 1 to Registration Transfers, along with the Rolls Royce it has been on for many years. Born on 16th October 1922, Bygraves is remembered by many for the famous radio programme Educating Archie and for TV's Singalongamax and Family Fortunes. His famous catchphrase was '*I wanna to tell you a story.*'

Impulse buy for GAZ

Cheryl and Gary Hopkins were not after a personalised number plate, but one presented itself to them one day. Cheryl says: "I spotted GAZ 22 in a Regtransfers advertisement in a colleagues national newspaper during my lunch hour. Just out of curiosity I'd looked to see if there were any registration numbers with my husbands initials. When I found GAZ 22, I couldn't resist it. Before I knew it we'd bought it! We had not been looking for a private plate and had not really talked about it. The right one just happened to be there. It's what you might call an impulse buy!"

Popular style TT marks

He's not an Audi TT driver and he's not been in a TT race - the reason Tony Talbot has bought 19 TT is simply for his birthday and initials. "It's not only for my initials, everyone calls me 'TT' as well. The 19 is for my birthday, 19th June. The new mark is proudly displayed on Mr. Talbot's new Mercedes. He runs a Financial Services company in Dudley, West Midlands.

Retirement collection

Malcolm Roger Haworth decided to buy C1 MRH as a subtle alternative to the plate he already owned, ROG 80R. "I thought it was a bit more formal. I'd had ROG 80R for about 12 years and when I retired recently I wanted something more distinctive."

Roger was interested in having a personal plate for many years, and when it came to the time when he could afford it, his first choice was his name plate, but he also had other ideas: "I had my own company manufacturing rubber components and it did occur to me to put plates on the company vehicles, but I never quite got around to it. We did buy FIL 444 for our son Philip though, for when he turned 21. He is very pleased with it. ROG 80R is now on my wife's Fiat Coupe, and my new plate is on my Jaguar Sovereign."

A plate for L16 ETY belle

When Liberty Peek was just 21 months old, her Nanny and Grandad saw a number plate for sale which looked like their Grandaughter's name. They decided to buy L16 ETY as an investment for young Liberty. Mum and Dad, Michelle and Lance Peek decided that perhaps it wasn't too early to let Liberty use the plate, so they put it on her toy car! Michelle said: "She is four now so she is too big for her play car but not quite big enough for the real plate yet! The plate is on my car at the moment."

Loopy about Lupo's!

When the new VW Lupo was launched in the UK, Richard and Anne Heather didn't waste much time ordering their first new car. Richard said: "We wanted something to make it a bit out of the ordinary. A personalised number plate seemed a good way, so I contacted Regtransfers to see what they had available. As luck would have it, when I asked if they had any plates with LUP in the registration, I was offered L1 UPO for a very reasonable price. Not wishing to sound too pleased (just in case the price went up!) I paid the deposit over the phone. I am very pleased with my Lupo and its matching L1 UPO plate."

The Heathers' then bought their second car, a VW Beetle. It was a trip down memory lane for them, Richard said: "Our very first car was an old VW Beetle, back in the early 1970's, when they had stopped production of the car. So when VW announced the new Beetle we put our names on a waiting list. It took nearly 2 years for it to be delivered, in the meantime we found S50 BUG!"

Chocs away!

Hanson's Chocolates in Lincolnshire has some chocs that will
be preserved for ever! – the number plate C11 OCS.
Jan Hanson who started the business from his home 16 years
ago said: "I thought of the idea of chocs for a number plate and
wondered if it was possible to get. Six months later I was
browsing through the Regtransfers number plate adverts and
saw C11 OCS. Local people comment on the plate all the time,
it makes them chuckle!" Jan is now planning to use the plate to
advertise his company.

Plate changes meaning all the time!

When Raymond Ratcliffe saw the number plate RMR 778, he knew that
it was what he had always wanted. Raymond said: "We'd been looking
for these initials for some time and could have bitten your hand off
when the advert appeared. When my wife is around the plate signifies
Ray and Margaret Ratcliffe, but when she can't hear me it represents
Raymond Melvin Ratcliffe! The reaction of other people is very
favourable and they appear to show great interest in its significance.
I tell them that its meaning changes depending whether the wife is with
me or not!"

Search for 'genuine' Orkney number proves fruitful

Now living in England, Chris Burrows from Orkney, has found a true Orkney number plate after an extensive search. Chris said: "As a Scot married to an Englishman and living in England, I still feel that "home" for me is in Orkney, where I spent my childhood. Orkney is the group of islands lying off the north coast of Scotland beyond John O'Groats. In the late 60's I bought my first car in Orkney. It was a dark blue Vauxhall Viva, registration number BS 7629. The BS registration has always been assigned to Orkney, and because the population is relatively small and very stable, most of the cars there still carry the local registration, or did until the new format was introduced last year. It therefore has very strong associations with home for me.

While waiting for delivery of my Mercedes SLK, my husband suggested that we should put a personal plate on it. Not wanting to have my name or initials on my car my first thought was that it would be fun to find BS 7629.

An enquiry to DLVA established that it no longer exists. It may well have ended up as a rusting heap on some forgotten corner of Orkney, or been pushed over a cliff when the car got too old, a common way of disposing of old cars on a remote island. So we started to look for a similar BS registration. The DVLA were very helpful and suggested that they could construct "7629 BS" for me, but I wanted a "genuine" one, and Orkney never had the reversed format with numbers before letters – there were not enough cars! So we spent a whole winter reading lists in newspapers and on web sites while I waited for delivery of the SLK. Eventually we found BS 7625 with Regtransfers and I decided that was near enough to do. It has been on my SLK ever since and I have become very attached to it. I have no doubt that I will keep this number now and that even if I end up driving something completely different from the SLK, it will still be registered BS 7625."

Women's motor racer preserved on a plate

Margaret Blankstone-Schoiber motor-raced for over 40 years. She has owned the number plate 345 MAB for about the same amount of time. Margaret said: "Just before my first husband Peter retired from owning a garage, we had decided to treat ourselves to a number plate each. Sadly he died, but I decided to go ahead and at the time MB 48 was the only MB number I could find. If I had any idea then that I would re-marry, it might have been different, but having motor-raced for over 40 years, I will always be Maggie B. I have now purchased 38 WS for my new husband, Wolfgang."

Feeling miffed

While waiting 16 weeks for their new MGF, David and Barbara Winsey from Southampton thought that they would search for a personalised registration number. David said: "Having dismissed the obvious 'MG' plates, we found one of interest - M11 FFY. Our son Philip, who's a new driver, said he wouldn't be seen in a car with that registration! So obviously we just had to get it! Muffy was the name of the tormented dog in the Bette Midler film Ruthless People. We also have R1 BUG for a Beetle (currently on retention certificate) and H18 EAN (High Bean - my nickname) on a Tigra."

Norman Wisdom's old plate finds its way into menswear

Sir Norman Wisdom owned the number plate 1 NW from 1958 to 1982. A famous photo of him in the book The Concise Guide to Car Numbers by Tony Hill shows Sir Norman in the boot of an 'S' type Bentley, with the plate 1 NW showing below him.

The plate is now owned by Neil Warwick, Director of Warwick's Menswear in Northants. The family collection also includes JW 65, OW33, WCW 2, 1 DNW and NW 230. Neil is very interested in finding additional NW numbers.

Part exchange number plate set

Nigel Hedges is the Area Secretary of the Bournemouth and Poole MG Owners' Club. His interest in number plates is as strong as ever. "In 1983, I was offered 1846 MG by a local dealer for £350 – a considerable sum for me at the time. My friend told me, 'if you don't buy it, you'll always regret it.' He was of course, quite right. Another friend at the time refused a running Alfa Romeo with the plate GGK 1T (he already had WBK 1T and WDK 1T) It was a wonder he didn't buy Gee – Gee KIT especially as he is a Saddler!

Soon after, I was offered 4542 PX by an MG contact in Southampton who was disposing of his Hillman Minx. He wanted £100 for the plate. I bought it and put it on my new MG Metro. I was delighted to have two cars with 'special' plates. It certainly took people's eyes off the rust of the MGB and the MG Metro never aged either! Four numbers and two letters has always been my favourite configuration.

When we bought the Rover Cabriolet, I asked DVLA for 4245 PX to match 4542 PX. I thought it would make a nice 'double-take' pair. DVLA were quite dismissive, initially asking me why I wanted the plate. They told me that 4245 had never been issued and that I couldn't have it. I wrote and said that surely 4245 would have been issued before 4542… I received no reply.

I turned to Regtransfers who were successful in finding 9176 PX for me at just £700, quite a bit cheaper than those listed today. The PX has no particular meaning for me except that it was the first cheap plate that started a set. I have always wanted EL or RU which are both Bournemouth numbers. PX is for Portsmouth, to which I have no affinity whatsoever.

When someone asks me why I have a PX number I just say that it stands for Part Exchange (in the trade)."

A very well travelled plate

Joseph Dewar from Fife in Scotland purchased UJD 777 from Regtransfers back in 1985. Joseph said: "At that time it was for a Datsun Stanza. After that it was on an Alfa Sprint, Nissan Sunny, Micra, Rover 213, Rover 216, Austin vp, Mercedes, Bluebird, BMW, Proton Alfa Estate, a Corsa then back to a Merc, so it really has been well travelled!"

Joseph, who was with The Royal Scots Greys for 22 years, retired in 1986. A member of the Registration Numbers Club, Joseph has attended almost 20 RNC and CNDA rallies around the country over the years. Joseph said: "I haven't attended the rallies for three years now due to my wife's illness, but I will be at the RNC rally at Stanford Hall, Leicester, this year. We were married in 1946 and we're still going strong after 55 years."

Like father, like son

William Ogilvie Dewar says that his first involvement with cherished numbers was when he purchased a new motorcycle, a Suzuki G5450E in 1988. "The registration number was E133 RWD, the WD was very fitting for my initials! I mainly used the motorcycle for touring, so I soon nicknamed it 'Roaming William Dewar'. My Father, who has the cherished number UJD 777, is a long-standing member of The Registration Numbers Club, and I attended many rallies with him. We would travel to them in his car, and my young daughter would come with us. The rallies were great fun, but of special interest to me was the significance and history of other owner's cherished numbers."

William eventually found his own cherished number, A1 WOD, which won 1st Prize in its class at the RNC Rally at Harewood in 1998. "I sold the Marbella in April 2001 and transferred A1 WOD onto a new Nissan Micra, which promptly won a second in class award, again at Harewood in June 2001."

Perhaps a plate for
Robot Wars 'Ming'

Andrew Cotterell from Somerset found the great name plate,
COT 1S to adorn his Jaguar XJ6. Andrew also has the plate
12 VET on a Corvette, but he is now selling this through
Regtransfers.co.uk. Andrew's hobby is taking part in the BBC's
Robot Wars programme with his team and their Robot called
Ming. Andrew says he wouldn't mind getting a plate saying
Ming! Andrew and his team are already World Tag Team
Winners.

Regtransfers.co.uk

No ordinary number

Edna and John Ireland from North Yorkshire said that when they bought their new Cosworth, the previous owner wanted to keep the number which he had on it so they had to find another one. Edna said: "As my husband's name is John and the previous number was K7 we thought K77 JON was appropriate for a car like a Cosworth rather than having just an ordinary number. We think that it makes the car look special and it is my husband's pride and joy."

A number one plate

Anthony Harold Worwood from Birmingham chose the number plate N14 AHW because 14 is his birth date and AHW are his initials. "Another reason I like this number is that it can be read as No. 1 4 (for) AHW."

Boy plate wins award

Kevin Scott, a Registration Numbers Club member from Nottinghamshire is very proud of the award his number plate has won. Kevin says: "I actually got the award for just missing out on first and second place by one vote! It was in the category – Names with/without date letter. I have been interested in number plates for quite a few years. I often used to read through the numbers for sale in the Regtransfers advertisements and did toy with the idea of buying KEV 130Y for a while. After saying that I couldn't afford it, my niece said to me 'Go for it, it would suit you, 'cos you're like del boy and it would look great on your van!' (I had a yellow Maestro van at the time.) Anyway I bought it and now it's on my Merc and it has given me many years of pleasure."

"I have been offered 5 times the amount that I paid for it but it's not for sale at the moment. I have tried to buy a couple more plates since but I have never found one that I liked better than mine although I would like to know who owns KEV 80Y!"

Filby plate proves a hit in Norfolk

Alan Filby was lucky enough to buy his name on a plate some ten years ago, but F1 LBY is also the name of a village in Norfolk. Alan said: "The Villagers show a lot of interest in the plate and I have had many offers of purchase. I have also been asked many times if the number is genuine." The photograph shows Alan outside Filby Restaurant in Filby Village.

"I was stopped by the Police on a very busy M6 one day, to be told by a young female constable that the spacing was incorrect. *'JOBSWORTH'* When I got home I checked it and it isn't. I have four sons all with cars who would love to own this plate. Also my nine brothers and four sisters would like ownership of it."

Nice one G1 DDO

When Neil Giddings was going to start his software services business, friends suggested he use his nickname Giddo as part of the name, so the business became known as Giddo Software Services.

Neil saw the number plate G1 DDO and thought it would add the finishing touch to his business car. Neil said: "The plate which displays my company name has helped my business greatly. People notice me more now by the plate. I have had managers from different companies making good remarks about it. I hadn't realised how effective it would be for marketing my company, it makes the car look fantastic and pays for itself too. I received an excellent service from Regtransfers in finding my personal plate."

Goosey, goosey gander

Simon Gander from Bickley in Kent has found the perfect plate for the nickname that he has had since he was at school - 'Goose'. He saw the number plate GOO 5E, but it was sold at auction for £14,000. Simon said "I had been looking for quite a long while, then I found G10 OSE at Regtransfers. It was much cheaper than the other plate and just as good since it is a bit more subtle. Everyone calls me 'Goose' except my mother and my wife Sarah." Sarah's plate is S8 SJG (for Sarah Jane Gander) and her birthday is on the 8th June.

"Goosey, goosey, gander
Where shall I wander?
Upstairs and downstairs
And in my Lady's chamber.
There I met and old man
That wouldn't say his prayers;
I took him by the left leg
and threw him down the stairs."

Four generations signified in special plate

For the Webster family, having the initials WW on a number plate is the ultimate way to signify four generations of Webster's. Graham William Webster said: "I have the plate P2 GWW on my car. At the moment we have four generations living that have a christian name followed by the names William Webster. There is my Father aged 83, myself aged 52, my son aged 29 and my grandson aged 3. This makes an excellent talking point when I receive a reaction from my friends and also people who see my GWW plate."

An unforgettable number plate

John C. Sturrock says he has never been very good at remembering his number plate. This prompted him to contact Regtransfers to see what they had available. John said: "They found V6 JCS for me which is very appropriate indeed. The V6 is for the car it is on - a Rover 75, which has a V6 engine, and JCS for my initials. I believe that everyone thinks about having a personalised number plate at some time. At least I won't be forgetting mine anymore!"

Surname plate hunted down

James (Jim) Miller had been searching for a number plate for a long time. When he finally found MIL 6742 he was very pleased. He said: "I wanted a number plate with my surname and this was the nearest I could get to Miller, and it was a very reasonable price too."

Rugby plate looks smart

"A great plate for a rugby player", says Don Kenyon who owns the number plate R4 GBY. It currently adorns his Smart Car, but he is hoping to sell it and says he has already had interest from a top Rugby player.

A long wait for a number plate!

Karen Pavin from Swansea says that a long time ago she saw the number plate PAV 1N but couldn't afford it. She was delighted to see it on the market again with Regtransfers several years later, and this time she had the money so had to buy it. Karen said: "It is a great plate for me, everyone comments on it." It is currently on Karen's Mazda MX-5.

RAC is a noticeable number

Catherine Craig from Glasgow says that the number plate
purchased for her husband, 2 RAC, is really obvious – RAC are
his initials, Robert A. Craig. "Number 2 was the best number we
could find at the time, but we're still looking for
1 RAC or RAC 1." Catherine's own number is CHC 790.

Family treble

Roy Ronald Drouet searched for many years for the right number plate to fit his initials. He was delighted when he finally found RRD 3. Roy said, "When my eldest son Ryan Roy became a driver, he also wanted a personalised plate. I was lucky enough to acquire 3 RRD at auction for him. My wife Dee then decided that she wanted a personal plate, and we found 333 DEE for her. It was doubly good because the numbers follow suit with my plate and Ryan's plate."

Trinidad number turns heads

Andrew Ramroop from Harrow, Middlesex was very pleased when he found the number plate H2 OMA for his wife, who is called Oma.

Andrew said: "I had been looking for a personal registration with my wife's name for a long time. When I first saw H2 OMA I couldn't believe my luck and it was so reasonably priced. The wife of the Prime Minister of Trinidad and Tobago is also named Oma, so as Trinidad nationals, when my wife and I are attending official functions, there are many peering eyes into our car to see if it is really 'she'! The personal registration certainly attracts much admiration and envious glances." Andrew is now on the look out for a number for himself.

Sensibly priced number

Joanne Lesley Mottram from Derby wanted a number plate at a 'sensible' price and was pleased when she found one with Regtransfers. Lesley said "I didn't want a number with a letter prefix, I wanted a dateless registration, so when I saw the plate JLM 805, which is my initials, I had to get it - it matched just what I was looking for. I don't regret buying it, in fact I enjoy having it on my car as it makes it feel more personal."

Just a Miget

Jimmy Kaleth had wanted a number plate for some time. Jimmy said: "I mainly wanted one because I thought it would look great on my rare Rover Mini Cabriolet - which it did ! I also thought it was a very good plate for the price."

Dedicated follower of number plates

Steve Waldenberg is a founder member of the RNC and has been Hon. Organising Secretary since about 1986. Steve said: "My interest in cherished numbers stems from the time that I had NW 6666 and 6666 NW on two of my cars. Alex Jackson, the originator of the RNC had a print and copy shop close by my town centre (Leeds) and when he set up the RNC back in 1977, he approached me for my assistance. I've been 'on the committee' so to speak since then!"

"The NW numbers were sold off when the bank manager came out of the cupboard and demanded his overdraft back. That was when the stock market tumbled in 1987. I did maintain ownership of cherished numbers with my two classic cars, the Jowett Javelin pictured here and a Jowett Bradford Van, GBL 889. The Javelin KTM 111 is a prize-winning example, this particular car being originally owned by the Jowett Agent in Bedford, Alf Thomas. After being abandoned for some 15 years, it was meticulously rebuilt to concours, and finished in time for the Javelin's 50th anniversary of introduction in 1997. This example dates from 1952."

"I also have HLZ 2489 on my Nissan Prairie, my daughter is called Hilary, but everybody calls her Hils, so this is the nearest number applicable to her name. HIL 5 would be nice though! My 'other' car is a 1969 Triumph 1300 and this has my initials (and birthday!) SIW 2846. Thank goodness for the Irish when your middle name begins with an I !"

Mirrored number plate 'worth every penny'

Timothy Evans from Essex saw the number plate S200 OTE on a car at a Honda Club Meeting some time ago and thought that it was the ideal number plate for him, "My car is a Honda S2000 and TE are my initials. Of course I couldn't have this plate because it belongs to someone else, but I started to keep my eyes open for something similar. When I saw S200 OOS in a Regtransfers advert, I thought it was even better than S200 OTE, so I got straight on the phone. I couldn't believe how reasonable the price was!"

The number is made up of an S, 2 and two noughts, then the letters OOS. Timothy says, "It's a great plate because it is a mirror of itself which ever way you read it, even in the rear view mirror. People are always commenting on how good it looks. I always tell them where I got it from – they can't believe how cheap it was either! I would say that three quarters of the Honda Club Members have S2000 plates. I think mine really stands out from the rest. It is definitely worth every penny."

A life-long interest in personal plates

Rod Lomax is the Publicity Officer for the Registration Numbers Club. He said "My interest in vehicle number plates started, I suppose, when I was a boy. As so many youngsters used to do before modern technology was invented, I collected car numbers in the fifties. It was a great thrill in those days to be the first to spot a new series and being brought up in Bury, Lancashire with the EN series was especially exciting as so many of them made names - BEN, KEN, LEN etc."

"My first car was a Hillman Imp way back in 1964 which was registered UEN 524. I remember visiting the Bury Motor Vehicle Taxation Office looking to obtain a much better number, but of course, this procedure had just finished round about that time and I was dismissed with a derisory wave of the hand. Being an apprentice at that time and running a car left me with no spare cash with which to purchase a cherished number, even at sixties prices."

"Twenty years passed by, marriage, a mortgage and all the other things associated with modern living, and it wasn't until 1984 that my interest in cherished plates was once again fired up. I had just bought a 3 litre V6 Ford Capri - a superb car, automatic transmission, lovely smooth performance and happened to notice 59 JRL for sale. I'd just started my own advertising agency after being made redundant from the multi-national I worked for and thought that this number would really add to promoting my own business."

"In the following years I searched for a matching number to grace my wife, Alison's car - her initials of AML unfortunately clashing with Aston Martin Lagonda - every one we saw for sale was extortionately priced. In 1989 I was lucky to see NEN 555 for sale... the only relevance being that it was, of course, a Bury plate where both of us had been brought up and it was a nice number. This was duly purchased and transferred to her Ford Sierra."

"1991 saw me purchase J5 JRL to add to the collection. As this was before the advent of retention certificates, I purchased a Jawa scooter to register the number to. I remember it arrived in a large flat packed box and was a self assembly job."

"In 1997 the 'R' prefixes came out and I had always promised myself that I would try to purchase R10 MAX. I called and called and called again, but it was four days before I finally got through to the DVLA call centre. As you will probably have guessed, the number had already gone - to this day I'm not sure whether it had been sold or had been held back for a future Classic sale. I was disappointed, but bought R40 MAX and R70 MAX as the next best thing. With an open '4' the first does look like LOMAX. These two are currently on retention certificates. I may eventually sell R70 MAX though as I'm running out of vehicles."

"The final (to date anyway) part of the story ends with me realising that a '5' and an 'S' are very similar and to make up a pair with 59 JRL, I managed to buy S9 JRL which currently resides on a Peugeot 106 1.5 litre diesel ... a pool car used by both my wife and her mother."

"I'm always on the look out for other good JRL numbers but they seem to be few and far between. On a recent holiday in Cornwall (where the RL series belongs) I spotted J509 JRL on a parked vehicle ... a coincidence you might think, but only one of many that have happened since I started on my collection almost twenty years ago."

Ego boosting number plates!

Michael Farquharson from Birmingham certainly knows how to stand out from the crowd with the number plates POV 17Y and M4 EGO!

Michael said: "I bought POV 17Y from a Mercedes owner in 1995. The amazing thing is that this was the number that the car was originally registered with in 1982 at a Mercedes dealership. I can't believe no one noticed the irony of this plate being on such a top range car. It is now on my Porsche 928 and the looks I get from people are quite something – you can see from their faces exactly what they are thinking! Which is exactly why I got the plate, its such fun." Michael says that he may even put it on his Ferrari later in the year – imagine the looks he'll get then. "M4 EGO is on my Ferrari at the moment, which also creates great interest. It looks just like 'My Ego'. Driving around in a Ferrari is brilliant, you get everybody looking all the time, firstly because it's a Ferrari, but then they see the plate and that finishes them off! It says it all! As a Numbers Dealer, some numbers I've got in my collection are BRA 61T (the opposite to POV 17Y) A1 8TUD, B7 TCH, M777 CKS and M77 CKY."

Plate is a safe bet!

Mr. Kelvin Jones decided to buy a number plate to mark his 30-years as a bookmaker. Kelvin said: "999 BET is a really good looking number for my business 'BetterBet' in Coventry. I'd been looking out for one with BET, so was very pleased when I came across this one. I've currently got the plate on my Mercedes."

All the OOOO's

Gavin Oakley from Worcestershire found the number GOO 100 at Regtransfers.co.uk. Gavin said: "I have always been interested in number plates and this one really caught my eye. As my initials are G.O. I thought they would be 'rounded off nicely' with the 100 after them. Also I feel that it will be worth more in the future.

A few weeks ago I was sitting in a car park in Droitwich when a car stopped behind mine. The driver and a young boy got out and I heard the boy say that he liked the plate. The driver said that it must be illegal having four 'O's in it. Thank goodness it isn't!"

Unforgettable plate for REM!

Roberta Moody from Worthing in West Sussex had thought for a long time that she would like a personal number plate. She said: "I first became interested in the idea of a personalised plate years ago when I visited the US and saw some of the amazing plates on the cars there; some of them were such fun and it was then that I thought that one day I would like one of my own. The real impetus to get one, however, was finally down to the fact that I was simply hopeless at remembering my own number plate – each time I changed my car it was always the same sad story – and so I decided it would be fun to have a plate with my initials on it. This surely would be IMPOSSIBLE to forget! The trouble was that my initials are REM – also the name of the pop group – which made any purchase of such a plate a rather expensive business.

"I saw an REM plate advertised in the Telegraph under one of Regtransfers listings and rang to find out how much it would cost. Needless to say it was a bit out of my league but the helpful sales person, Justine, found M500 ODY for me instead which was a nice surprise and certainly close enough to my surname for me to never forget it. It was also far more affordable."

"One thing I hadn't thought about before buying the plates is how often you are recognised by friends and workmates when you are out driving around with personalised plates on your car. It is surprising how many times you get noticed in the unlikeliest of places!"

WAR 6S collection

In 1989, Malcolm Ward purchased his first personalised number plate, WAR 6S. Although it could look like wars, Malcolm says that at a distance it really looks like his surname. "Several months later I was glancing through the adverts, when what should I spy but WAR 61S which is still a reasonable likeness if the 1 is considered an apostrophe. The sight of these together certainly makes many do a second take."

Several years later Malcolm found the plate M7 SVV, which looked like all his initials (MJSW). "The complete collection cost under £1,000 in total. I realise that M7 SVV will have no appeal or value to anyone else, but I obtain immense pleasure from it."

Y1 PEE for 5 UES plate

Sue from Warwickshire was going to buy Y1 PEE
but took advice and decided to buy 5 UES instead.
That was just twelve months ago. Now Sue is
selling her plate because she says, her husband
isn't keen on the attention it draws. Now she will
have to look for one that is a bit more discreet!

U.A.E plates are a subtle choice

Keith and Enid Hughes from Wrexham, North Wales wanted a pair of plates for an unusual reason. Keith said: "My wife and I worked in Sharjah, United Arab Emirates for nine years and we thought it appropriate to use the Sharjah Airport identification letters SHJ, for our personal cars in the UK. We are pleased with our registrations – SHJ 916 is my number, on a Mercedes C180 and SHJ 798 is Enid's number and that is on a Citroen ZX. Only those who have worked in Sharjah will recognise the initials SHJ – it was only our former colleagues that knew what the plates meant. We wanted subtle plates, so I came up with this meaning - one that most people wouldn't understand, I certainly didn't want a number with my initials KH."

'Bond' plate for 007 fan

Adam Kaye from London has scooped probably the most sought after number plate for any James Bond fan – 8 OND. Adam collects all types of 007 memorabilia, and this is a highly prized addition to his ever-growing collection. Adam said: "I just wanted to own it. I have been a Bond fan since I was a child and have been collecting books, photographs, models etc. ever since."

Regtransfers had offered the plate to the filmmakers at Pinewood Studios, to help promote the 20th Bond film 'Die another day' which is currently in production, but the same afternoon, Adam rang up and bought it! Adam says he would be very pleased if 8 OND was used for publicising 'Die another day'.

Award winning number plates

Stephen William Latimer from Bath purchased SWL 9 in 1978 to match the reverse issue, which he also owns. Stephen said: "It is on the car which has been in the family since new. The licensing office found it amusing that I was transferring a registration number to, and not from a Morris Minor! I have amassed twenty one awards at the thirty three car numbers rallies that I have attended since acquiring the mark 9 SWL. It has adorned eleven cars since 1976 when the transfer fee was only £5. I have been a member of the Registration Numbers Club since 1977."

Fire fighting father and son plates

Phill Davison is a fire fighter in Spennymore, County Durham, where he has been based for three years. He was very pleased when his parents bought him a private registration for his 21st birthday on 25th January 2002. Phill said: "The number plate DAV 999C was a lovely surprise. Unfortunately though, my wonderful Father died of a heart attack last November at the age of 45. He was also a fire fighter and was in charge at Darlington fire station. His registration reads DAV 999V, which is now on my Mum's Land Rover. Having a similar surname plate as my Dad's makes it even more special to me now that I have lost him."

'U' numbers with historic value

Geoff and Judith Peace are Registration Numbers Club members from Wigan. They have an excellent pair of 'U' plates, which, says Geoff, they chose for their historic value. "U 4678 is an early Leeds registration - one of the first issued with a single letter at the beginning."

"In common with several other authorities, Leeds issued two parallel series with the result that until the system was changed in 1920, the same registration could be carried by a car and a motorcycle. Following research, I discovered that the car registration was cancelled on 28 March 1934, earlier records having been lost."

"The motorcycle registration survived on a 1920 Redrup Radial – one of only three manufactured by Charles B. Redrup of Leeds. It was restored and took part in the 1986 Banbury Run and went on to be displayed in a museum in Hampshire. Subsequently it was sold overseas and the registration was transferred. My wife holds 8190 U on a Peugeot 106 originally issued by Leeds on 14 March 1958 to a Ford Popular."

Geoff says his Father was in the Garage trade and remembers the outcry from some people when the number plate system was first introduced. Comments like "I'm not having a number on my car!" were apparently not unusual!

How to be treated like Royalty...

An exquisite pair of number plates have been found by David and Wendy Bramley from Nottingham, for their Bentley and BMW. David said: "I was looking in the paper one Sunday when I saw 1 WMB in a Regtransfers advert. I thought that this number was perfect for Wendy as her initials are WMB. A couple of weeks later we were on holiday and I woke up one morning and suddenly thought – that plate is BMW backwards! What a coincidence when the plate is on a BMW as well!"

"I saw my own number plate 1 DBE, in a daily newspaper. It really fitted the bill with my initials being DB with the E for 'Engineer'. I was so lucky to get it. I had it on a Granada at first and one day I went to see a customer at an oil company. The parking attendant was just directing someone into the last parking space when I arrived. He bent over and looked at my plate, then called the man out of the parking space and off to an overflow car park and waved me into the space instead!"

Boarding school nickname sticks like mud

If you met David Clay you could be forgiven for not realising that David was his real name! Since he was at boarding school he has been known as Ebb! David said: "The nickname derived from my surname 'Clay', which first became 'Muddy', then, because the ebb tide leaves mud behind, the nickname evolved into 'Ebb'! My wife, Valerie found the number plate 47 EBB and gave it to me as a surprise present. It fits the bill perfectly especially as the 47 is part of my postcode and STD code." David had already purchased 774 VAL for Valerie. The 774 also signifies part of the telephone area code and postcode.

Number plate wish is fulfilled

Donald English from Nottingham was very pleased to find the number plate 4 DE with Regtransfers. Donald said: "I have always thought that one day I would get myself a personalised number plate, but every time the money got used for more needy things.

One day I was driving home from Nottingham City when I noticed that the car in front of me had the plate 1 DE. I was behind it for about twenty minutes. I had already ordered a new car, now I had to have a personal number as well.

In the Daily Express on March 18th 2000, Regtransfers had an advert showing 2000 DE and 4 DE and in other papers 41 DE and 71 DE. I enquired about them all. Number 4 is our house number and of course DE are my initials. Of the four companies I contacted Regtransfers sales person Laura was the most professional in the way she dealt with my queries etc. Once I decided on 4 DE it all went like clockwork. My family, friends and mostly my three teenage Grandchildren think the number and car are super."

Austin 7 reunited with original plate

Michael Aplin couldn't believe it when he saw his car's original number plate up for sale. Michael said: "I bought my Austin 7 1930 Box Saloon in 1997 when she had an age related number plate. The then owner had made enquiries and discovered that the original registration number was WP 55 which, coincidentally, I saw for sale with Regtransfers at the same time. Unfortunately it was on the market for several thousand pounds, which I considered excessive and did not pursue the matter further, though I regularly checked on it and saw that it remained for sale over the following year. During this time I also made enquiries which confirmed that my car had originally been registered in Worcester under the number WP 55.

Twelve months later I noted that the number was no longer advertised and I regretted bitterly that the opportunity to reunite my car and her original number had been lost – probably forever. However, four weeks later I noticed that the plate was for sale again, though at an increased price. I rang the following morning and purchased this very special number!

Since then the re-uniting of my classic car with her original number plate has brought considerable pleasure to my wife and I, though at the expense of our childrens' inheritance! Now that both car and number plate have been re-united, they will never again be parted whilst they remain in our possession."

Keeping it in the family

The Holmes family from Devon have an outstanding collection of number plates, one of which has been featured on television. Graham Holmes said: "My wife, Elaine Dorothy Zena has the number plate EDZ 1 for her initials, my son has A1 MCH standing for his initials (Matthew Christian Holmes) and my daughter, Hayley Rebecca has HR 11. Hayley also has JAZ 6872 representing her first car (a Honda Jazz) and her birthday – 6/8/72. Matthew also has FF 7819 on his Ford Focus. This registration was not bought especially but was on a Morris Minor we purchased, only realising afterwards the F.F. connection.

Matthew's birthday is 25 December, so of course he owns 25 DEC as well. It is on his MR2 and has been featured on TV's Top Gear programme." Graham says that he is the only one without a plate! "Trouble is that would mean getting yet another car!"

Delicious D8 NUT's on a plate

Enjoying a couple of plates of donuts is Nichola Bentley from
East Sussex. Nichola said: "I have been in the Donut business for
about eight years, attending some of the biggest events in the
country, so I was particularly happy when I managed to acquire
the number plates D8 NUT and D10 NUT. D8 NUT is on my new
VW Beetle and D10 NUT is on my lorry and catering unit.
Having number plates runs in the family - my Father's number
plate is BRE 4D, which he acquired 20 years ago. He had it on his
lorries when he had a chain of bakeries in the south of England."

Go dog lover! Go dog lover!

Christine Purcell from Surrey says there were two reasons for wanting the number plate A9 DOG, "I am a Radio Amateur with callsign GO DOG. I am also an avid lover of dogs and have three rescue mongrels, Razzle, Goofie and Monkey. I have been asked before if I am from Barking! Someone also said once that the plate should have been K9 DOG, but I couldn't afford that and in any case my van is too old. I have seen children look at the plate and the 'I Love my Dog' stickers and smile."

Chinese '8' makes plate lucky

Mark Hawkins chose the number plate 8 MH firstly because these are his initials and secondly because he says it is a good investment. "I feel it is something that is personal to you for life. It has enhanced every vehicle that I have put it on. I often get stopped by Chinese people interested in the number because in their culture the number 8 is very lucky!" (This is because eight sounds like the Chinese word for 'Good Fortune'.)

Isle of Wight plate

David Woodhouse was born and bred in Lake, on the Isle of Wight. He now lives a quarter of a mile away. David says that DL letters have been assigned to vehicles on the Isle of Wight for as long as he can remember. "DL has now been replaced with the letters HW (for Hampshire and Wight). This is why I wanted one of the old numbers. I had DL 8905 years ago on a motorbike and WDL 312 on a van, which I sold for £15 scrap! I wish I'd kept the numbers because they are going to go up in value now that the new system has come in. My son has one of the new numbers, HW51 DLD which I don't think looks so good really."

Wedding present for Madonna

Nigel Lowe, A & R boss at London based 'Cry Records' says he was looking forward to going to Madonna's wedding to Guy Ritchie on 22 December 2000. He even bought the pop queen a personal number plate as a wedding present - MAD 75. Nigel said: "MAD is short for Madonna, however, it was never given to her as I wasn't invited to the wedding as expected."

Family of number plates

The Ginns family from Leicestershire have an excellent collection of number plates, for instance, Gerald. F. Ginns has the number plate GFG 242. Gerald said: "This number represents my initials and the number of the house where my wife Janet was born and brought up in Scraptoft Lane in Leicester, so it is very appropriate! The plate FG 999 is my daughter's plate. Her name is Fiona Ginns - it suits her very well. It was my late father's number (Frank Ginns), and was passed down to me, but I always wanted a GFG registration and thanks to Regtransfers I now have one.

My wife's Honda has the registration ABC 999. It was on my late mother's car for many years. The Leicester City Council have ABC 1 on the mayoral car and they always wanted our number, but as a free gift - they didn't want to pay for it or even get her another personal number!"

Cherished in memory

Sharon McKenna from Essex wondered if it was possible to find a number plate spelling the name Frank, in memory of the dear husband she lost to cancer last year. Their daughters, Anthea, Nicole and Veronica began an intensive search on the Regtransfers website and soon came up with F12 ANK. Sharon said: "Frank worked hard all his life and the girls and I wanted to find something that we could cherish in his memory. We've never had personalised number plates before but F12 ANK really fulfils our wish. The number plate will be kept in the family now and passed down to our daughters.

"'La Riche' was Frank's business - making the hair dye that Punk's use - he actually invented *Directions* hair colour. Frank drove around in his favourite car - an Aston Martin and a friend of ours has painted a picture of it onto the wheel cover on the back of our Mitsubishi Shogun. Our Grandson Luc Frank Aston McKenna has even been named after Frank and the Aston Martin! Everyone around here knew Frank and is pleased to see him remembered with the number plate and the painting. It certainly makes the car very important to us – Frank was a very special man."

His and hers plates

Margaret Gillies had always fancied getting herself a personalised number plate, but as she changed her car every three years she didn't think it was worthwhile. When Margaret retired though, she decided that now was the opportune time. Margaret said, "I purchased 5913 MG as a retirement gift to myself, M.G. being my initials. Then I bought GIL 3603 for my husband George for his birthday, GIL representing Gillies. George had wanted a Classic Mercedes for a long time, so when he eventually got round to purchasing one I knew he would appreciate having personalised number plates as well."

Good plates for ducks!

The Silcock family from Cornwall have an association with water that has gone a bit further than most with the purchase of a pair of number plates that any self respecting ducks would be proud to own!

Ex-Marine diver Roger Silcock is a professional ocean yachtmaster whilst his son, Ewan has a degree in marine leisure management and teaches sailing and wind surfing.

"There is definitely a 'water' connection in this family. My daughter Adrienne has a degree in tourism and also loves wind surfing. I thought these were an excellent pair of plates, better than getting their initials. The children's Grandparents left them some money in trust. I decided to invest that money for them in these number plates. I think it has been a far better option than stocks and shares." Roger has had an interest in number plates from when he was a child. "We used to collect numbers as a kid, from 1 to 100. We always knew to get the number one plates from the foreign embassies such as CAN 1 for Canada. I'm not aware that WET 1 was ever a diplomatic number plate though!" The Silcock family own a couple of other personalised plates, but WET 1 and 1 WET definitely stand out. "When we do sell them on they'll have to go as a pair. I just wish we owned some ducks!"

A very important number plate

Andrew Thomson from Fulmer in Buckinghamshire bought one of the most prestigious plates on the market today. Andrew said: "I was off to play rugby one morning when I saw it advertised in the newspaper. I just had to get it, I admit it was a bit of an impulsive buy!" The plate has pride of place on Andrew's Ferrari, "It looks great - so over the top, but my girlfriend says it looks really tacky!"

Andrew is now keen to sell this 'very important person' plate. VIP 1 was first issued for the Pope's visit to Ireland in 1984. It is an Irish mark and should not really have been allowed into the British system. It once got a mention in the Guinness Book of Records for being the highest price asked for a registration number.

Wise old owl

Lesley Avis from Essex has collected owls for several years. Every type of ornament, soft toy or replica of an owl is around Lesley's house. When she decided that she wanted a personal number plate, only an 'owl' would do! "I was very pleased to find J6 OWL. It is on its second VW Polo now. I'm often spotted by friends and family when I am around town in the car."

25th wedding anniversary plate

A treasured car received a treasured plate on the Ramsdale's 25th Wedding Anniversary. Mallory Ramsdale from Dunstable, Bedfordshire, bought the number as a present for her husband Tony to celebrate their quarter of a century together. "It was the perfect partner for his pride and joy, a Jaguar TWR XJ40. Cars have always played a large part in our lives so it was an appropriate present for him."

272

The sight and sound of a Scorpion

Tony and Gill Burgess from Worthing, West Sussex purchased a matching pair of initial plates. Gill said: "In May 1999, my husband and I ordered the car of his dreams, a Grinnall Scorpion – a three-wheeled sports car powered by a 4 cylinder, 1100cc BMW motorbike engine. These are made individually by a small firm in Bewdley, Worcestershire. As a birthday present I wanted to give him a personalised number plate based on his name, Anthony Michael Burgess. The first one that we chose from Regtransfers was on a donor car that unfortunately then failed its M.O.T. As the low numbered 'C''s were just being released and C1 AMB was rather expensive, we thought that C3 would be just right for the three-wheeled car.

Two months later, I exchanged my old Polo for a nearly new one. I too had always wanted a personalised number plate. As my name is Gillian Margaret Burgess, I was really pleased to find that C3 GMB was still available, to match C3 AMB.

In October 1999 we drove up to Worcestershire in my car to collect the Scorpion from the factory. The journey home was quite an experience as the sight and sound of a Scorpion really turns heads.

Sadly and unexpectedly my husband passed away in January 2000. Nevertheless we had such happy motoring times together, especially in the Scorpion and we were so proud of our matching number plates."

Pug's are my little treasures

Peter Jackman from Anglesey loves Pugs and really wanted a number plate that had 'PUG' on it. Peter said: "I chose A800 PUG because it was the cheapest PUG plate Regtransfers had on offer. I cannot envisage life without my Pugs. Years ago I mated one of my little treasures, the idea being to sell the puppies to make some money. She had four pups, but they were so beautiful that I couldn't bring myself to sell them, so I ended up with six pugs! Although I don't believe in showing dogs, I do belong to the Pug Dog Club. I do on occasions go to a Pug Dog Show and have seen a plate PUG 1 which I understand belongs to one of the pug breeders."

The girl with everything

Gill Baker says that her daughter is the 'girl with everything'. "We weren't sure what to buy her for her 29th birthday, but when we saw the number plate AU51 ZOE, we knew that she would love it. We took Zoë with us to Australia two years ago, so 'Aussie Zoë' seemed appropriate. It is a brilliant plate and she is very pleased with it."

Tony Brooks driving at Oulton Park around 1957. He won the race.

Motor racer's winning number

On January 22, 1959, Britain's first Formula One World Champion, Mike Hawthorn, tragically died on the Guildford bypass. His Jaguar 3.4 spun out of control on the wet road after clipping a lorry. He hit a tree, and died at the scene.

He was 29 years old. His close friend Rob Walker, one of Formula One's racing team owners, who had also raced at Brooklands and Le Mans, was the only witness. Rob was driving his Mercedes as Mike overtook him at great speed. Rob's distinctive number plate ROB 2 would certainly have been recognised by Mike as he had approached the Mercedes.

Today, Rob Walker is a Journalist for the American magazine Road and Track. He also holds the number plate R8, whilst his wife Elizabeth has E53. Rob said: "In the late 1950's I used to ring up Birmingham issuing office and they would let me have virtually any plate that I wanted, except ROB 1 - that of course was reserved for the Mayoral vehicle. I acquired plates for friends and family too, including a JW plate for Johnnie Walker and ND 1 for my Father-in-law Mr. N. Duncan, (although it was later withdrawn as we found that it had already been issued to Lady Nora Docker, of the banking family). Around 5 years ago I saw R5 advertised for £100,000 and a few years before that I saw it advertised for £60,000. It is quite unbelievable how much number plates have grown in value. ROB 2 is on an Alpha 156 these days. On that fateful day, the plate was on a 300SL Mercedes Gull Wing, that could get up to a speed of 150 mph."

Since writing this piece, Rob Walker sadly died on 29th April 2002.
Our thoughts are with his family.

Joe goes with the flow

Joseph Randlesome, Business Development Manager at Regtransfers bought the number plate J10 OES as all his friends and family call him Joe. "I was working out combinations for clients who wanted their name on a plate and suddenly I'd worked one out for me. I knew that it was a good investment opportunity as well as being a great plate. I'd been dealing with number plates day after day, but hadn't thought of what I could get for myself. It's the kind of plate that might not be obvious at first but if you know me you can see it says 'Joes'. I really love it and I've just put it on my new BMW."

A nickname to remember

Jason Manning, a salesman at Regtransfers.co.uk was delighted when he secured the number plate M19 NNO because he says it looks just like 'Manno', which has been his nickname since he was very young.

Idle by name, but not by nature!

Dean Lawrence Easterby, a long-standing Registration Numbers Club member from Longton, near Preston has been interested in number plates from the age of around 15. He bought his first number plate, when he was just 18 years old. Dean said: "I had just passed my driving test and purchased a Mk. 4 Ford Cortina with the Irish number plate MIA 8508. The car soon became known as Mia. In 1981 my mother and I bought a Rolls Royce – a 1969 Silver Shadow. A friend had 5 YOO and on seeing another YOO plate it appealed to me."

Later that year, Dean bought a 1963 Austin Cambridge, which had the number plate 4 G00. Dean liked the number because of its similarity to his YOO plate. Then came the purchase of the ultimate plate for Dean. "I had always wanted a number with my initials and in 1984 when I was 21 years old I was lucky enough to see DLE 1 advertised. I decided then to start looking for the reverse plate 1 DLE. This took 15 years! It is an excellent plate that not only has my initials, but also spells 'idle' – which incidentally, I am not! - I can't imagine ever parting with any of these numbers - in fact I would sell absolutely everything before I'd sell my plates!"

The most looked at car around

Stuart Ogilvie from Edinburgh has owned the number plate POP 80Y for 15 years. "I am the plates second owner. It draws an unbelievable amount of attention - people take photos of the car and even leave stickers on it asking to buy the plate! I have had substantial offers for the plate over the years but never wanted to sell it. I have offered it to a great number of Record companies, Pop stars and famous people including Richard Branson and Chris Evans, but I'm holding out for the right price. I get special treatment wherever I go with this number on my car. My children, David, Stuart, Michael and Rebecca love going out in the car. POP 80Y was first issued on a Ford Fiesta, I have it on a Bentley Arnage T."

Plate worth more than the car!

John Witcombe from Wilmslow, Cheshire is pleased with his purchase of P8 JAG for his gold coloured Jaguar. John says: "The reason I fitted the plate was because I run up more miles than the average Jaguar owner (now coming up to 100,000 trouble free miles), and when selling a 6 year old car, I found that it was worth surprisingly little, mainly due to this high mileage. When P8 JAG became available for around £1,000, I thought that it would greatly assist me when selling the car, but now I have grown to like the plate and little did I know at the time that if I kept the car for a bit longer, the plate would be worth more than the car!"

"Warp 8 - engage!"

Richard Pearson from Lincolnshire, now living in Bedfordshire is a bit of a Trekkie to say the least! He has been interested in the science fiction programme Star Trek since he was a young boy of about 8. He first saw the cult program in Germany where he lived with his 'army' family for a couple of years. But it was when Richard moved to England in 1982 that he really became addicted: "I used to get home from school and watch the original series; then came The Next Generation, Deep Space Nine, Voyager and now the new Enterprise. I wanted a personalised number plate for my new Honda Accord and started thinking of what I could have that would relate to Star Trek. I was very pleased with myself for coming up with W4 RPB! I have had people stop me in the street and say they think it's a great plate.

It would be difficult to choose a favourite series, but if I had to pick one it would be *The Next Generation*. This was the first series where Warp 8 was mentioned – previously this speed was not possible. Captain Picard (my favourite character of this series) is the one who usually gives the order "set course ensign….warp 8….engage!"

Offer on the street for desirable number

Steve and Kathryn Baptist from Lancashire have a pair of number plates that are going up in value whilst they enjoy using them year after year. Steve said: "I came across 6 SB six years ago in one of Regtransfers adverts and decided to buy it at £8,000. Then I found KJB 99 for my wife, Kathryn Jeanne Baptist in one of Regtransfers brochures. Just recently I was approached by a man who said he had seen the plate a few times and really liked it. He offered me £18,000 for it! When I bought the plates I hadn't thought that they might have investment potential, but with 6 SB being a particularly short plate it is very desirable, more so now that the new style plates have begun. I couldn't have asked for more from my purchases and I will be watching their value with interest over the next few years."

A gem of a plate

My own plate had to be my name. I knew someone years ago that had an excellent name plate and I always thought that one day I would like to get my own. When I came to work at Regtransfers, I started hunting around for a suitable 'Ruby' plate, and soon found one - R11 BYJ. My parents christened me Ruby Jane. I was named Ruby after my Grandmother to whom I was very close, but my Mum preferred to call me Jane. They felt that they couldn't christen me Jane Ruby because it hadn't been long since Jack Ruby had shot Lee Harvey Oswald. Nevertheless I became known as Jane, which I always loathed. Being a rather determined little girl, at the age of seven I announced to everyone that "my name was going to be Ruby from now on" - and it has stayed that way ever since. Now I have the number plate to go with it!

Sporty car has to have a personal number

George Laidlaw from Kilsyth, near Glasgow says that his son had always wanted him to buy a personalised number plate. George said: "Unfortunately our son Harry died aged just 45. It was my wife Margaret who finally pushed me into getting the number plate 3 GLL, which represents my initials. We also got one for Margaret at the same time – R1 MBL. My plate is on a BMW Z3 and Margaret's is on a Peugeot 206 CC. I've always had sporty cars, but started out with motorbikes. The BMW wouldn't look right without a personal plate."

Impressive number plate

Terence McKenna says he chose the number plate TEL 395X because his Christian name is Terence and he is known as Tel. Terence says: "I also wanted to personalise my then new Mercedes C. Class Elegance. I find that people are amused and impressed when they see my plate."

Acting double

Actress, Emma Jane Hooper from Cornwall purchased the number plate J10 EJH for her sporty Mazda MX-5. "The plate has my initials, but also doubles up for my stage name Emma Jane Hartman. Over my career, I have been in some top shows on TV, such as Holby City, Birds of a Feather and Eastenders. I was so pleased with the way that Regtransfers dealt with my purchase – I didn't have to do anything, they did it all for me – even though it was a Bank Holiday – so a big thank you!"

50th Birthday Gift

"Being a devotee of the Volvo marque, I had always wanted a 480 Turbo Auto ever since they were introduced", says John Richard Aldous from Surrey, "Having found an excellent example (L plated) I was perfectly happy to spend the rest of my driving life cleaning and maintaining it. Imagine my surprise when my family presented me with L50 JRA on my 50th birthday this year, what a fantastic gift! My family inform me that I have Registration Transfers to thank, their service was second to none and I have no hesitation in recommending them to others who want to make their car a bit more personal.

A good reason to buy a car!

Peter Mayhew says that one of the reasons for buying his new car was that he'd found a number plate to go with it! C20 GTO matches the model of his Mitsubishi. "I think it looks really cool!" he said.

Remembering Peter

Judy Teader had wanted a number plate in remembrance of her husband. Judy said: "My daughter, Helen, gave me the number plate P1 JJT. The P stands for Peter, and the 1 means that he was number 1 – the best. JJT are my initials.

This number plate is a wonderful way of remembering my beloved husband, Peter, who was tragically killed in a gliding accident (which wasn't his fault) along with another pilot, on September 14th 2001.

It is such a happy way of remembering him and easy to find the car in a car park!"

Have you got a story to tell about your number plate? Contact Ruby at Regtransfers on 01582 606105 or email ruby@regtransfers.co.uk

Part Five
Lists and Addresses

Original Licensing Authorities - where plates were originally issued

Diplomatic Plates

DVLA Local Office addresses

Glossary of Terms

Useful Contacts and Addresses

Original Licensing Authorities

A	London	BR	Sunderland
AA	Hampshire	BS	Orkney
AB	Worcestershire	BT	Yorkshire E.R.
AC	Warwickshire	BU	Oldham
AD	Gloucestershire	BV	Blackburn
AE	Bristol	BW	Oxfordshire
AF	Cornwall	BX	Carmathenshire
AG	Ayrshire	BY	London, Croydon
AH	Norfolk	C	Yorkshire W.R.
AJ	Yorkshire	CA	Denbighshire
AK	Bradford	CB	Blackburn
AL	Nottinghamshire	CC	Caernarvonshire
AM	Wiltshire	CD	Brighton
AN	London West Ham	CE	Cambridgeshire & Isle of Ely
AO	Cumberland	CF	West Suffolk
AP	East Sussex	CG	Hampshire
AR	Hertfordshire	CH	Derby
AS	Nairnshire	CJ	Hertfordshire
AT	Kingston upon Hull	CK	Preston
AU	Nottingham	CL	Norwich
AV	Aberdeenshire	CM	Birkenhead
AW	Shropshire	CN	Gateshead
AX	Monmouthshire	CO	Plymouth
AY	Leicestershire	CP	Halifax
		CR	Southampton
B	Lancashire	CS	Ayrshire
BA	Salford	CT	Kesteven (Lincs.)
BB	Newcastle upon Tyne	CU	South Shields
BC	Leicester	CV	Cornwall
BD	Northamptonshire	CW	Burnley
BE	Lindsey (Lincs.)	CX	Huddersfield
BF	Staffordshire	CY	Swansea
BG	Birkenhead	D	Kent
BH	Buckinghamshire	DA	Wolverhampton
BJ	East Suffolk	DB	Stockport
BK	Portsmouth	DC	Teeside, Middlesborough
BL	Berkshire	DD	Gloucestershire
BM	Bedfordshire	DE	Pembrokeshire
BN	Bolton	DF	Gloucestershire
BO	Cardiff	DG	Gloucestershire
BP	West Sussex	DH	Walsall

DJ	St. Helens	FJ	Exeter
DK	Rochdale	FK	Worcester
DL	Isle of Wight	FL	Huntingdon & Peterborough
DM	Flintstone	FM	Chester
DN	York	FN	Canterbury
DO	Holland (Lincs.)	FO	Radnorshire
DP	Reading	RP	Rutland
DR	Plymouth, Devonport	FR	Blackpool
DS	Peebleshire	FS	Edinburgh
DT	Doncaster	FT	Tynemouth
DU	Coventry	FU	Lindsey (Lincs.)
DV	Devon	FV	Blackpool
DW	Newport (Mon.)	FW	Lindsey (Lincs.)
DX	Ipswich	FX	Dorset
DY	Hastings	FY	Southport
E	Staffordshire	G	Glasgow
EA	West Bromwich	GA	Glasgow
EB	Cambridgeshire & Isle of Ely	GB	Glasgow
EC	Westmoreland	GC	London
ED	Warrington	GD	Glasgow
EE	Grimsby	GE	Glasgow
EF	Hartlepool, West Hartlepool	GF	London
EG	Huntingdon & Peterborough	GG	Glasgow
EH	Stoke-on-Trent, Hanley	GH	London
EJ	Cardiganshire	GJ	London
EK	Wigan	GK	London
EL	Bournemouth	GL	Bath
EM	Bootie	GM	Motherwell & Wishaw
EN	Bury	GN	London
EO	Barrow-in-Furness	GO	London
EP	Montgomeryshire	GP	London
ER	Cambridgeshire & Isle of Ely	GR	Sunderland
ES	Perthshire	GS	Perthshire
ET	Rotherham	GT	London
EU	Breconshire	GU	London
EV	Essex	GV	London
EW	Huntingdon & Peterborough	GW	London
EX	Great Yarmouth	GX	London
EY	Anglesey	GY	London
F	Essex	H	Middlesex
FA	Burton upon Trent	HA	Warley, Smethwick
FB	Bath	HB	Merthr Tydfil
FC	Oxford	HC	Eastbourne
FD	Dudley	HD	Dewsbury
FE	Lincoln	HE	Barnsley
FF	Merionethshire	HF	Wallasey
FG	Fifeshire	HG	Burnley
GH	Gloucester	HH	Carlisle

HJ	Southend-on-Sea	KJ	Kent
HK	Essex	KK	Kent
HL	Wakefield	KL	Kent
HM	London	KM	Kent
HN	Darlington	KN	Kent
HO	Hampshire	KO	Kent
HP	Coventry	KP	Kent
HR	Wiltshire	KR	Kent
HS	Renfewshire	KS	Roxburghshire
HT	Bristol	KT	Kent
HU	Bristol	KU	Bradford
HV	London	KV	Coventry
HW	Bristol	KW	Bradford
HX	London, Middlesex	KX	Buckinghamshire
HY	Bristol	KY	Bradford
J	Durham	L	Glamorganshire
JA	Stockport	LA	London
JB	Berkshire	LB	London
JC	Caernarvonshire	LC	London
JD	London	LD	London
JE	Cambridgeshire	LE	London
JF	Leicester	LF	London
JG	Canterbury	LG	Cheshire
JH	Hertfordshire	LH	London
JJ	London	LJ	Bournemouth
JK	Eastbourne	LK	London
JL	Holland (Lincs.)	LL	London
JM	Westmoreland	LM	London
JN	Southend-on-Sea	LN	London
JO	Oxford	LO	London
JP	Wigan	LP	London
JR	Northumberland	LS	Selkirkshire
JS	Ross and Cromarty	LT	London
JT	Dorset	LU	London
JU	Leicestershire	LV	Liverpool
JV	Grimsby	LW	London
JW	Wolverhampton	LX	London
JX	Halifax	LY	London
JY	Plymouth	M	Cheshire
K	Liverpool	MA	Cheshire
KA	Liverpool	MB	Cheshire
KB	Liverpool	MC	London
KC	Liverpool	MD	Middlesex
KD	Liverpool	ME	London
KE	Kent	MF	London
KF	Liverpool	MG	London
KG	Cardiff	MH	London
KH	Kingston-upon-Hull	MJ	Bedfordshire

MK	London	OL	Birmingham
ML	Middlesex	OM	Birmingham
MM	London	ON	Birmingham
MN	Isle of Man	OO	Essex
MO	Berkshire	OP	Birmingham
MP	London	OR	Hampshire
MR	Wiltshire	OS	Wigtownshire
MS	Stirlingshire	OT	Hampshire
MT	London	OU	Hampshire
MU	London	OV	Birmingham
MV	London	OW	Southampton
MW	Wiltshire	OX	Birmingham
MX	London	OY	London
MY	Middlesex	P	Surrey
N	Manchester	PA	Surrey
NA	Manchester	PB	Surrey
NB	Manchester	PC	Surrey
NC	Manchester	PD	Surrey
ND	Manchester	PE	Surrey
NE	Manchester	PF	Surrey
NF	Manchester	PG	Surrey
NG	Norfolk	PH	Surrey
NH	Northampton	PJ	Surrey
NJ	East Sussex	PK	Surrey
NK	Hertfordshire	PL	Surrey
NL	Northumberland	PM	East Sussex
NM	Bedfordshire	PN	East Sussex
NN	Nottinghamshire	PO	West Sussex
NO	Essex	PP	Buckinghamshire
NP	Worcestershire	PR	Dorset
NR	Leicestershire	PS	Zetland (Shetland (Is.)
NS	Sutherland	PT	Durham
NT	Shropshire	PU	Essex
NU	Derbyshire	PV	Ipswich
NV	Northamptonshire	PW	Norfolk
NW	Leeds	PX	West Suffolk
NX	Warwickshire	PY	Yorkshire N.R.
NY	Glamorganshire	R	Derbyshire
O	Birmingham	RA	Derbyshire
OA	Birmingham	RB	Derbyshire
OC	Birmingham	RC	Derby
OD	Devonshire	RD	Reading
OE	Birmingham	RE	Staffordshire
OF	Brimingham	RF	Staffordshire
OG	Birmingham	RG	Aberdeen
OH	Birmingham	RH	Kingston upon Hull
OJ	Birmingham	RJ	Salford
OK	Birmingham	RK	London, Croydon

RL	Cornwall	TL	Kesteven (Lincs.)
RM	Cumberland	TM	Bedfordshire
RN	Preston	TN	Newcastle upon Tyne
RO	Hertfordshire	TO	Nottingham
RP	Northamptonshire	TP	Portsmouth
RR	Northamptonshire	TR	Southampton
RS	Aberdeen	TS	Dundee
RT	East Suffolk	TT	Devon
RU	Bournemouth	TU	Cheshire
RV	Portsmouth	TV	Nottingham
RW	Coventry	TW	Essex
RX	Berkshire	TX	Glamorganshire
RY	Leicester	TY	Northumberland
S	Edinburgh	U	Leeds
SA	Aberdeenshire	UA	Leeds
SB	Argyleshire	UB	Leeds
SC	Edinburgh	UC	Leeds
SD	Ayrshire	UD	Oxfordshire
SE	Banffshire	UE	Warwickshire
SF	Edinburgh	UF	Brighton
SG	Edinburgh	UG	Leeds
SH	Barwickshire	UH	Cardiff
SJ	Buteshire	UJ	Shropshire
SK	Caithness	UK	Wolverhampton
SL	Clackmannanshire	UL	London
SM	Dumfrieshire	UM	Leeds
SN	Dumbartonshire	UN	Denbighshire
SO	Morayshire	UO	Devon
SP	Fifeshire	UP	Durham
SR	Angus	UR	Hertfordshire
SS	East Lothian	US	Glasgow
ST	Inverness-shire	UT	Leicestershire
SU	Kincardineshire	UU	London
SV	Kinrosshire	UV	London
SW	Kirkcudbrightshire	UW	London
SX	West Lothian	UX	Shropshire
SY	Midlothian	UY	Worcestershire
T	Devonshire	V	Lanarkshire
TA	Devonshire	VA	Lanarkshire
TB	Lancashire	VB	Croydon
TC	Lancashire	VC	Coventry
TD	Lancashire	VD	Lanarkshire
TE	Lancashire	VE	Cambridgeshire & Isle of Ely
TF	Lancashire	VF	Norfolk
TG	Glamorganshire	VG	Norwich
TH	Carmarthenshire	VH	Huddersfield
TJ	Lancashire	VJ	Herefordshire
TK	Dorset	VK	Newcastle upon Tyne

VL	Lincoln	WS	Leith
VM	Manchester	WT	Yorkshire W.R.
VN	Yorkshire N.R.	WU	Yorkshire W.R.
VO	Nottinghamshire	WV	Wiltshire
VP	Birmingham	WW	Yorkshire N.R.
VR	Manchester	WX	Yorkshire W.R.
VS	Greenock	WY	Yorkshire W.R.
VT	Stoke-on-Trent	X	Northumberland
VU	Manchester	XA-XF	London
VV	Northampton	XG	Middlesborough
VW	Essex	XH	London
VX	Essex	XJ	Manchester
VY	York	XK-XP	London
W	Sheffield	XR	London
WA	Sheffield	XS	Paisley
WB	Sheffield	XT-XY	London
WC	Essex	Y	Somerset
WD	Warwickshire	YA	Somerset
WE	Sheffield	YB	Somerset
WF	Yorkshire E.R.	YC	Somerset
WG	Stirlingshire	YD	Somerset
WH	Bolton	YE	London
WJ	Sheffield	YF	London
WK	Coventry	YG	Yorkshire W.R.
WL	Oxford	YH	London
WM	Southport	YJ	Dundee
WN	Swansea	YK-YP	London
WO	Monmouthshire	YR	London
WP	Worcestershire	YS	Glasgow
WR	Yorkshire W.R.	YT-YY	London

Diplomatic Plates

Normal Format Marks, specially assigned to heads of missions, etc . Below are all those seen in the past three years, specifically last seen in 01/99 to 01/00 by 1903 AAT members. [●] , 02/00 to 01/01 [blank] or 02/01 to 01/02 [◀].

BG 1	Bulgaria ◀	**BOS 1A**	Bosnia ◀
IC 1	Iceland ◀	**BOT 1**	Botswana ◀
NL 1	Netherlands ◀	**BRZ 1**	Brazil ◀
NL 2	Netherlands	**CAN 1**	Canada
NZ 1	New Zealand	**CDA 2**	Canada
NZ 2	New Zealand ●	**CDR 1**	Congo Democratic Republic
PE 1	Peru ◀	**COL 1**	Colombia
RI 1	Indonesia ◀	**1 CZE**	Czech Republic ◀
SF 10	Finland ◀	**DOM 1A**	Dominica ◀
VG 1	Victoria, Australia	**ELS 1**	El Salvador ◀
WA 1	Western Australia	**FIJ 1**	Fiji ◀
1 M	Malaysia ◀	**FGN 1**	Nigeria ◀
1 BE	Belgium ◀	**FRA 1**	$ France
1 CF	Commonwealth Foundation ●	**GYA 1**	Guyana ◀
961 CH	Switzerland (Confederation Helvetia)	**HSL 1**	Sierra Leone ◀
1 CY	Cyprus ◀	**IND 1**	India ◀
1 EC	Eastern Caribbean	**ITA 1**	Italy
1 EE	Ethiopia ◀	**JPN 1D**	Japan ◀
1 MO	International Maritime Orgn	**MAU 1**	Mauritius ◀
1 PY	Paraguay	**MEX 1**	Mexico ◀
1 RF	Russian Fedn ◀	**NEP 1**	Nepal
1 RL	◀	**NIC 1**	Nicaragua
1 SL	Sri Lanka ◀	**OMA 1N**	Oman ●
1 TT	Trinidad ◀	**PAN 1**	Panama ◀
ADE 1	Adelaide, Australia ◀	**PHI 1**	Philippines ◀
ALG 1A	Algeria ◀	**QLD 1**	Queensland, Australia
ANG 2	Angola ◀	**QTR 1**	Qatar ◀
ANU 1	Antigua	**QUE 1**	Quebec, Canada ◀
AUS 1	Australia ◀	**RWA 1A**	Rwanda ◀
BAH 1	Bahrain	**SEY 1**	Seychelles
BDH 1	Bangladesh	**SGP 1**	Singapore ◀
BDS 1	Barbados ◀	**SLO 1A**	Slovenia
BEL 12E	Belize	**SPA 1N**	Spain ◀
BOL 1	Bolivia ◀	**SUD 1**	Sudan ◀

SVK 1A	Slovakia ◄	**1 MLT**	Malta
THA 11	Thailand	**1 MLW**	Malawi ◄
TUN 1	Tunisia ◄	**1 MOZ**	Mozambique ◄
UDM 1	Uzbekistan	**1 MRN**	◄
UKR 1	Ukraine ◄	**1 MYN**	◄
ZAM 1	Zambia ◄	**1 NAM**	Namibia ◄
ZIM 1	Zimbabwe ◄	**1 NAU**	Nauru
		1 NBD	Brunei ◄
		1 NWY	Norway
1 ARG	Argentina ◄	**1 OES**	Austria ◄
1 BLS	Belarus ◄	**1 PAK**	Pakistan ◄
1 BMS	Bahamas ◄	**1 PER**	Iran ◄
1 CAM	Cameroon ●	**1 PNG**	Papua New Guinea ◄
1 CZE	Czech Republic ●	**1 POL**	Poland ◄
1 DAN	Denmark	**1 POR**	Portugal ◄
1 ECU	Ecuador ◄	**1 RCI**	Ivory coast ◄
1 EST	Estonia ◄	**1 RKF**	Dominican Republic ◄
1 GAM	Gambia ◄	**1 ROA**	Armenia ◄
1 GER	Germany ◄	**1 ROK**	Korea ◄
1 GRC	Greece ◄	**1 ROM**	Romania ◄
1 GRG	Georgia ◄	**1 RSA**	South Africa ◄
1 GRN	Grenada ◄	**1 SCN**	St Kitts Nevis
1 HRV	Croatia (Hrvatska) ◄	**1 SLU**	St Lucia ◄
1 JAM	Jamaica ◄	**1 SVE**	Sweden ◄
1 KEN	Kenya ◄	**2 SVG**	St Vincent & the Grenadines
1 KSN	Kazakstan ◄	**1 SZD**	Swaziland
1 KYR	Kyrgystan	**1 TAN**	Tanzania ◄
1 LEB	Lebanon ◄	**1 TON**	Tonga ◄
1 LES	Lesotho ◄	**1 TUR**	Turkistan ◄
1 LIT	Lithuania ◄	**1 UAE**	United Arab Emirates ◄
1 LUX	Luxembourg ◄	**1 UGA**	Uganda ◄
1 MAG	Hungary (Magyar) ◄	**1 VCN**	Vatican
1 MAK	Macedonia	**1 VEN**	Venezuela ◄
7 MLD	Maldives ◄	**1 VNA**	Vietnam ◄

Glossary of Terms

RT	Regtransfers
CC	County or City Council
CNDA	Cherished Numbers Dealers Association
RNC	Registration Numbers Club
LO	Local Office (DVLA)
DVLA	Drivers Vehicle Licensing Agency
DVLC	Drivers Vehicle Licensing Centre (term used before DVLA)
AFRL	Automatic First Registration and Licensing
VRO	Vehicle Registration Office
LVLO	Local Vehicle Licensing Offices
SR&O	Statutory Rules and Orders (of Northern Ireland)
V778	Retention Certificate
V750	Certificate of Entitlement
V5	Registration document
V317	Cherished Transfer application form
Retention Certificate	Certificate to show who has the right to hold the number
Grantee	The person(s) or company (referred to on a retention certificate) who has the right to assign the mark to a vehicle
Nominee	Third party who also has the right to assign to a vehicle agreed by the grantee

Local Vehicle Registration Offices in England & Wales

Aberdeen
Greyfriars House
Gallowgate
Aberdeen
AB10 1WG
01224 648 216

Bangor
Penrhos Road
Penrhosgarnedd
Bangor
LL57 2JF
01248 351 822

Beverley
Crosskill House
Mill Lane
Beverley
HU17 9JB
01482 887 884

Birmingham
2nd Floor
Edward House
Edward Street
Birmingham
B1 2RF
(0870) 240 3518

Bournemouth
Tregonwell Court
118 Commercial Road
Bournemouth
BH2 5LN
01202 558 531

Brighton
4th Floor
Mocatta House
Trafalgar Place
Brighton
BN1 4UE
01273 692 271

Bristol
Northleigh House
Lime Kiln Close
Stoke Gifford
Bristol
BS34 8SR
0117 969 2211

Cardiff
Archway House
77 Ty Glas Avenue
Llanishen
Cardiff
CF14 5DX
02920 753 355

Carlisle
Ground Floor
3 Merchants Drive
Parkhouse
Carlisle
CA3 0JW
01228 539 401/2

Chelmsford
2nd Floor
Parkway House
49 Baddow Road
Chelmsford
CM2 0XJ
08702 412 147

Chester
Norroy House
Nuns Road
Chester
CH1 2ND
01244 348 195

Coleraine
County Hall
Castlerock Road
Coleraine
BT51 3HS
028703 41461

Dundee
Caledonian House
Greenmarket
Dundee
DD1 4QP
01382 225 765

Edinburgh
Dept. of Transport
Saughton House
Broomhouse Drive
Edinburgh
EH11 3XE
0131 455 7919

Glasgow
46 West Campbell Street
Glasgow
G2 6TT
0141 226 4161

Inverness
Longman House
28, Longman Road
Inverness
IV1 1SF
01463 239321

Ipswich
Podium Level
St Clare House
Greyfriars
Ipswich
IP1 1UT
01473 258451

Leeds
1st Floor
42, Eastgate
Leeds
LS2 7DQ
0870 240 3514

Lincoln
Firth Court
Firth Road
Lincoln
LN5 7WD
01522 543 681

Luton
2, Dunstable Road
Luton
LU1 1EB
0870 240 3515

Maidstone
Coronet House
11, Queen Anne Road
Maidstone
ME14 1XB
0870 240 3517

Manchester
Trafford House
Chester Road
Manchester
M32 0SL
0870 241 2146

Newcastle-Upon-Tyne
Eagle Star House
Regent Farm Road
Newcastle-upon-Tyne
NE3 3QF
0191 284 1026

Northampton
Wootton Hall Park
Northampton
NN4 0GA
01604 762 131

Norwich
11, Prince of Wales Road
Norwich
NR1 1UP
01603 616 411

Nottingham
Block 6
Government Buildings
Chalfont Drive
Nottingham
NG8 3RA
0870 241 1876

Oxford
Ground Floor
3, Cambridge Terrace
Oxford
OX1 1RW
01865 724 056

Peterborough
88, Lincoln Road
Peterborough
PE1 2ST
01733 551 671

Portsmouth
5th Floor
Baltic House
Kingston Crescent
Portsmouth
PO2 8AH
023 9263 9421

Preston
Fulwood Park
Caxton Road
Fulwood
Preston
PR1 9NZ
01772 793 912

Reading
77-81 Basingstoke Road
Reading
RG2 0ER
0870 241 5161

Sidcup
12/18 Station Road
Sidcup
DA15 7EQ
0870 240 3516

Sheffield
Cedar House
Hallamshire Court
63, Napier Street
Sheffield
S11 8HA
01142 722 236

Shrewsbury
Whitehall
Monkmoor Road
Shrewsbury
SY2 5DR
01743 366 422/350 511

Stanmore
Government Building
Canon Park
Honeypot Lane
Stanmore
Middlesex
HA7 1BD
0870 241 1269

Stockton
St. Marks House
St. Marks Court
Thornaby
Stockton on Tees
TS17 6QR
01642 796 600

Swansea
Heol Pentre Felen
Swansea
SA6 7HG
01792 783 900

Truro
Pydar House
Pydar Street
Truro
TR1 2TG
01872 278 635

Wimbledon
Ground Floor
Connect House
133-137 Alexandra Road
Wimbledon
SW19 7JY
0870 600 6767

Worcester
Clerkenleap Barn
Broomhall
Worcester
WR5 3HR
01905 821 720

Useful Contacts and Addresses

Beaulieu National Motor Museum
Montague Ventures Ltd
John Montague Building
Beaulieu
Brockenhurst
Hampshire
SO42 7ZN

Tel: 01590 612345
Fax: 01590 612624
email: info@beaulieu.co.uk

Backstage Fancy Dress
14, Larkspur Close
Fields End
Hemel Hempstead
HP1 2HP

Tel: 01442 252334
Fax: 01442 248182
email: maxsecunda@btconnect.com

Brocket Hall
Welwyn
Hertfordshire
AL8 7XG

Tel: 01707 335241
Fax: 01707 375166

The Registration Numbers Club
Hon. Organising Secretary:
Steve Waldenberg FSCA
R.N.C. Office
P.O. Box MT12
Leeds LS17 7UD

Tel: 0113 226 7497
Fax: 0113 226 1110
email: organisation@registrationnumbersclub.org.uk

Stondon Transport Museum
Station Road
Lower Stondon
Henlow
Bedfordshire
SG16 6JN

Tel: 01462 850339
Fax: 01462 850824
email: info@transportmuseum.co.uk
www.transportmuseum.co.uk

1903 And all that
Newsletter (quarterly)
Covers all aspects of vehicle registration
For a sample copy and subscription details
send a large S.A.E. to the editor:
John Harrison,
175 Hillyfields
Loughton
Essex
IG10 2PW

Driver & Vehicle Licensing Agency
Swansea
SA6 7JL

DVLA Customer enquiries: 01792 772134

Cherished Numbers Dealers Association (CNDA)
201 Great Portland Street
London
W1N 6AB

Tel: 01788 538301